"Turn to the piece entitled 'Inspirational Romance' and begin reading. You may begin mumbling to yourself, 'This is so good. . . . This is *wonderful.*' Then you'll settle into the steady expectation of delight. Such is the charm of Paul Willis's splendid essays."

—JOHN WILSON, editor, *Books & Culture*

"Even readers who know nothing about mountain climbing will find these essays compelling for their humor, their deft description, and the fierce love of place that inspirits them all. No simplistic, spiritualized nature metaphors here. Instead, Willis gently deflates empty religiosity, all the while vividly depicting the forbidding mysteries and dangers of the mountain wilderness that slowly transform the soul."

—DEBRA RIENSTRA, associate professor, Calvin College, and author, *So Much More: An Invitation to Christian Spirituality*

"*Bright Shoots of Everlastingness* takes us on a journey of the best kind—an absorbing, honest, and always entertaining wander through the wonders and struggles of a life spent in realms that matter so much: mountains, literature and friendship. Through it all, under Willis's self-revealing hand, we sense our own fallenness, and with him, we reach upward for grace."

—LESLIE LEYLAND FIELDS, author, *Surviving the Island of Grace,* *Surprise Child,* and *Out on the Deep Blue*

"How did the twin austerities of churchly religion and mountain climbing produce such a wise, lyrical, generous-spirited, fall-down funny, and profoundly human voice as the one we hear in each of Paul Willis's stunning essays? I know you will like this voice. You will trust it when it is poking gentle fun at its own sacred cows, and yours, because you will feel its warm heart, and you will follow willingly as it takes you deeper into yourself and into the mystery and the beauty of the human spirit."

—DOUG FRANK, professor, The Oregon Extension of Houghton College

BRIGHT SHOOTS
of
EVERLASTINGNESS

To Kevin + Mercy,
With thanks for you!
Paul   Nov. 2005

BRIGHT SHOOTS
of
EVERLASTINGNESS

*Essays on Faith and
the American Wild*

PAUL J. WILLIS

WORDFARM
LA PORTE, INDIANA

WordFarm
2010 Michigan Avenue
La Porte, IN 46350
www.wordfarm.net
info@wordfarm.net

Scripture quotations are variously taken from the Authorized and Revised Standard Versions of The Holy Bible.

Cover Image: iStockphoto

Design: Andrew Craft

USA ISBN-10 0-9743427-7-7
USA ISBN-13 978-0-9743427-7-1
Printed in the United States of America
First Edition: 2005

Library of Congress Cataloging-in-Publication Data

Willis, Paul J.
  Bright shoots of everlastingness: essays on faith and the American wild /
Paul J. Willis.-- 1st ed.
    p. cm.
  ISBN-10: 0-9743427-7-7 (pbk.)
  ISBN-13: 978-0-9743427-7-1 (pbk.)
  1. Willis, Paul J., 1955- 2. Evangelicalism--United States. 3. Christian biography--United States. 4. Mountaineers--United States--Biography. I. Title.
  BR1643.W55A3 2005
  277.3'0825--dc22

                                                                    2005008315

P 10 9 8 7 6 5 4 3 2 1
Y 12 11 10 09 08 07 06 05

to my father,
David Lee Willis,
and in memory of my mother,
Earline Louise Willis

Acknowledgments

MY HEARTFELT THANKS to the following people who have helped with one or more of these essays in various ways: Sam Alvord, Andrew Craft, David Downing, Christine Felton, Leslie Leyland Fields, Doug Frank, John Gallagher, Al Haley, Linda Lawrence Hunt, Jack Leax, Kate Maynard, Marilyn Chandler McEntyre, David Oates, Steve Roper, Mark Eddy Smith, Heather Speirs, Dave Willis, John Wilson, and Jim Zoller.

And my love and thanks to my wife, Sharon, and our all-too-grown-up children, Jonathan and Hanna, without whom I would have been in no kind of shape to write any of this stuff.

My thanks as well to the editors of the publications in which some of the essays in this book first appeared, sometimes in different versions:

Ascent: The Mountaineering Experience in Word and Image (Sierra Club Books): "The Kahiltna Open"

Books & Culture: "The Wardrobe Wars"

The Climbing Art: "Whitney at Forty: An Alzheimer's Expedition"

The Cresset: "Do You Want Some Company?"

Horizon: "A Wilderness Journal" (as "Beyond the Barranca: A Wilderness Journal")

Houghton Milieu: "Lattice Bridge Road"

Image: A Journal of the Arts and Religion: "Spokane: A Triptych"

Interdisciplinary Studies in Literature and Environment: "Development Dreams"

Moody: "All the Way Down"

OE Journal: "But Basney Says," "The Geography of Hope" (poem), and "New Seeds in California: The Contemplative Journals of John Leax"

The Other Side: "All the World" and "Care to Dance?"

Redwood Coast Review: "Accidental Admissions" (as "Hanging by a Thread")

River Teeth: "Bright Shoots of Everlastingness"

Summit: "SWAGS: The Next Generation" (as "The Next Generation")

SWAGS Newsletter: "Inspirational Romance" (as "The SWAGS Inspirational Romance")

Verve: "Manzana Schoolhouse" (poem)

Wind Row: "One Fine Morning"

Word Tastings (Santa Barbara Review Publications): "On Being and Becoming a Mountaineer" (as "Mountaineer")

"All the World" and "On Being and Becoming a Mountaineer" also appeared in *OE Journal.*

"Manzana Schoolhouse" also appeared in my chapbook *Poison Oak* (Mille Grazie Press).

"Spokane: A Triptych" also appeared in *The Best American Spiritual Writing 2004* (Houghton Mifflin) and will appear in *The Best Christian Writing 2006* (Jossey-Bass).

"The Wardrobe Wars" also appeared in *The Lamp-Post: A Literary Review of Lewis Studies* and in *The Best Spiritual Writing 1999* (HarperSanFrancisco).

Contents

But felt through all this fleshly dress
Bright shoots of everlastingness

—Henry Vaughan, "The Retreat"

Introduction

THESE NARRATIVE AND REFLECTIVE ESSAYS, written over the past twenty-five years, have been revised and fitted to form a rough composite of two loves and how I have grown into them. The first and foremost love is for the God of my evangelical youth. The second, related love is for the mountains of the American West.

All true loves are full of quarrels, and these essays tangle through some of mine. American evangelicals are no doubt some of the tackiest, corniest, pigheadedest people on earth. However, they are my people, and I am one of them. By historical accident or design, they are the unsavory husk for the kernel of divine love that has been given for me to taste. The mountains, too, have proven themselves difficult company. As objects of a climber's obsession, they have provided physical harm and spiritual disappointment. But as sacramental gift and presence, they have offered a steady joy.

Some readers may regard these twin enthusiasms for Christian faith and mountain wild as rather contradictory—or paradoxical at best. For most writers who treat these subjects do so by graduating from one to the other. John Muir, for example, leaves behind the fanatical beliefs of his father for a gospel of Yosemite. Allegiance to the God of the Scriptures is left behind to embrace the truer spirit of the wilderness. This is the pattern that pervades much of our nature writing today—writing that I have greatly loved—and it is not my role to critique it. I trust that each writer struggles in good conscience to tell the truth about the given mysteries of his or her experience. I only wish to attempt the truth about mine. So far, the God of my youth has not gone away. He—or she—still roams the peaks and meadows of memory and imagination. A brother of mine, asked to describe my first novel, came up with this: "Narnia comes to the American wilderness." And it keeps on coming.

It occurs to me, then, that I may have assembled a book without an audience. Evangelical Christian readers may find all of the unabashed belief and delight in alpine wilderness a bit puzzling, if not heretical. And my "wilderness" readers may scratch their heads at the seriousness with which I take the Scriptures and the intimate God they impart. Part of me is John the Baptist; part of me is John Muir. Or, rather, all of me is both.

Taken together, the essays of course are not about "all of me." Much is missing. Friends and family, students and strangers briefly appear, then disappear, hesitating in the margins like understudies behind the curtain, not quite certain of their cues. The social world that accounts for so much of who we are is not consistently realized in the essays that follow. Those *dramatis personae* that do appear have often been given fictitious names to protect them from my habits of gross caricature. For what I have both said and not said about all who have touched and bordered my life, some of you very dear to me, I ask forgiveness.

And these essays, at their best, may not be "about me" at all. The paradox of the essay form, and of that endless egoism which has fueled the common essayist from Michel de Montaigne to E. B. White, is that the more I recount about myself, the more you discover about your own experience. As I blather on about my own grandmother, you awaken to the presence of yours. If the thing is done correctly, my grandmother exits the stage quietly and yours steps forward in passionate soliloquy, leaning into the audience and leaving you collapsed and weeping there in the front row, your seatmates wondering what has come over you. But these moments cannot be promised, and you, dear reader, will in fact be stuck for long stretches with my meager self playing its part upon a rather bare stage. In the end, however, I hope you will find your own mountains rising up out of that stage, whatever shape they may take for you, and behind and within them, the wild Lover of our souls.

THE SHORE

Even before a word is on my tongue,
lo, O Lord, thou knowest it altogether.

—Psalm 139:4

Bright Shoots
of Everlastingness

"I WAS SAVED FROM SIN when I was going on thirteen. But not really saved." That is the beginning of a well-known chapter from Langston Hughes's autobiography, *The Big Sea*. In this chapter he keenly recalls a revival meeting in his Auntie Reed's Kansas church. The people moan and the preacher shouts until every one of the children on the mourners' bench in the front row has jumped up and come to Jesus. Every last one, that is, except Langston and a boy named Westley. But the pressure builds and Westley crumbles, whispering to Langston, "God damn! I'm tired o' sitting here. Let's get up and be saved." Then Langston alone is left. Finally, he too cannot resist the beseeching of the minister and the frenzied attention of the church. So he gets up, to the joy of his Auntie Reed and all present. But Langston is disappointed in his own lie, and also in the failure of Jesus to make his presence known as promised. That night he cries, because he doesn't believe there is a Jesus anymore.

So when Langston Hughes says that he was saved from sin at a young age, he is being ironic. But I think I could say that I was saved at an early age with a fair degree of earnestness. And if it weren't for the cliché involved, I could say it with great confidence. One rainy Sunday morning in the damp basement of the Victory Bible Church in Marysville, Oregon, my mother presented all of us in the first and second grades with a choice. She held up two hearts made out of cardboard, the sort you might see in store windows just before Valentine's Day. Except these hearts were not red, not even a gauzy pink. Far from it. One heart was very white, and the other was very, very black. What we all had right now, she told us, were black hearts—black because of the sin in our lives. If we wanted a white heart, we would have to ask Jesus to give one to us. If we asked Jesus, and really meant it, and were truly sorry for all the bad things we had done, he would wash our black hearts with his red blood and make them white.

Here is where some confusion set in: *black + red = white*? What gives? Even I knew my primary colors and what happened when you mixed them, though I was nearly the worst in the second grade when it came to art. Black plus red would surely make something like—brown, maybe? Burnt sienna? That was one of my least favorite crayons, though I did like the exotic sound of the name as it appeared on the paper wrapping. So even then I realized that things worked differently at church sometimes than they did in school.

In the end, I put aside the alchemical question and focused on the outcome: that white heart. I realized I wanted one of those, I wanted to ask Jesus to replace my black one. In a similar way,

I believed I had heard our pastor, Dr. Bowser, assure us that we would all receive new bottoms in heaven. (New *bodies*, I now think it was.) I saw nothing much wrong with my present bottom, but it pleased me to imagine an assembly line in which God would slap on shiny new ones for everyone coming to glory. There was one time, though, I could have used a new bottom. I was playing in a nearby field and didn't quite make it home in time to unburden myself in the proper place. I was old enough to feel ashamed. To make matters worse, my brother took just that moment to persuade me to ride our bikes down to the library. My bicycle seat was a little extra cushiony that afternoon, and when we got to the library we hung around and read *Boy's Life* for a good, long, odorous while. Then we stopped to see my father at the university on our way home. He smelled something. I confessed. Patiently, and with much labor, he cleaned me up in his office bathroom. You might call it burnt sienna magically turned back into white. In any case, it was definitely an act of grace.

Bottoms, though, were mere accessories. What mattered was a good, white heart. So, one rainy afternoon, I quite deliberately lay on my bed, chin propped in both hands, and asked Jesus into my heart. I had to ask him *into* my heart so that he could get to work on the colors there, sort of like repainting a bedroom. And for all I know, he did. I was taught to believe that Jesus would do what he promised, whether I felt anything or not. I took my white heart on faith.

Perhaps in an effort to make my decision for Christ, as we called it, real to myself, I duly reported to my parents what I had done. They listened very patiently. My mother was encouraging, my father more—not neutral, but gentle about it. But it was my father I asked to go down the aisle with me for the altar call at the end of our next Sunday service. For even I knew, at age seven, that you couldn't just lie on your bed in the privacy of your own scuffed room and ask Jesus into your heart and expect that to count for something. What really mattered was what we called a public profession of faith.

Our sanctuary was a grand but decaying turn-of-the-century edifice with wooden pews on the main floor and theater seats in the balconies on three sides. At some point in my grade-school years I liked to stay after church and pick up extra bulletins in the balconies as a way of expressing my devotion. The Old Testament stories of the young Samuel serving in the tabernacle were stories I liked. And I liked the way that old room felt when it was empty, when everyone was talking on the steps outside. It was dim and quiet, and a midday breeze might ruffle the cheap red curtains behind the top rows of seats, and I could be alone there, picking up bulletins left on the floor.

The front of the church held a baptistry on one side and a large railed platform across the center, anchored by a wooden pulpit as solid and certain as the gospel. Behind the pulpit a choir loft, where my mother sang in a shiny green robe with a golden yoke, filled a light-green concave shell. On the back of this shell were no crosses or images of any sort, only a verse in gothic script from the Gospel of John: "We would see Jesus." There wasn't a picture of him or anything, just the hope that we would see him. When you think about it, a nice iconoclastic touch.

It was toward this pulpit, and toward this motto, that I solemnly walked with my father at the conclusion of the morning service. Dr. Bowser usually gave an altar call at the end of his sermons, but if I remember correctly, his invitation on this day was perfunctory. That didn't matter. I knew my time. I marched to the front, cheeks blazing with self-consciousness, and Dr. Bowser came down from his pulpit to meet me.

It was hard to imagine a kindlier man. As a child I had no living grandfather, and was always on the lookout for one. Dr. Bowser fit the description. Balding, with white hair, he had with children a merciful and vaguely patriarchal way. Yet he looked physically powerful, and the rumor was that he had played fullback on the football team at Wheaton College. I asked him about this once, and he laughed and said, "I played way back." Dr. Bowser learned to preach before microphones were commonly used, and as a result, he preached with prophetic power and volume, soaring in nineteenth-century oratorical cadences through the trials and tribulations of Israel in the wilderness, pleading with God in the person of Moses to deliver them to the Promised Land. When I thought of Moses, I gave him the face of Dr. Bowser. (And why was it we called him *Doctor*? If he was indeed highly educated, he did not wear it on his sleeve. When it came to teaching Sunday school, he always deferred to the scriptural knowledge of my father, who had several degrees from the Bible Institute of Los Angeles and had planned to be a teacher on the mission field before he turned to biology.)

I do not know what Dr. Bowser preached about on the morning that I came forward, but I do remember that after the service he took me to his shabby little study with a deacon or two, and that my father was left outside. He very directly asked if I believed that Jesus had died for me, if I intended to repent of my sins, if I wanted to love and follow Jesus beyond all others. And I said *yes, yes, yes,* barely getting the words out and nodding my head and wondering now what I was getting myself into. But I was a precocious reader and knew the story of Christian on his way to the Celestial City, and right now Dr. Bowser was the ragged old Evangelist, pointing the way to the narrow gate, and I knew I had to head that way, though at my age the journey might seem laughable and unlikely.

Then the questions were done and we all stood up, and out from the shadows behind me came a very old woman in black who had been there the whole time. Her presence greatly startled me. She held out before her in a gnarled hand a tract, I think, just like the wicked queen in *Snow White* who suddenly appears in front of you on that dark ride in Disneyland, an apple in her outstretched palm. Then the woman pronounced a severe blessing upon my head and disappeared. I had no idea who she was, and though I imagine her intentions were good—making sure of the new converts—I felt that I had somehow met a threatening presence hiding in the holy place.

Next on my pilgrim's progress—a few weeks later, I suppose—I was baptized at an evening service. I entered the baptistry from behind in a robe of white on small steps that curved down into the water. Dr. Bowser was already there in a black robe, specially equipped with waders. My white robe did not want to go underwater at first, floating up around the edges. But I damped it down and stood docilely at my pastor's side, facing the darkened congregation. It was an odd feeling, standing there in warm water up to my chest, as if I were at the shallow end of the public pool, and looking out on everyone else, dry as can be in their pews—the women in dresses, the men in slacks and shirts and ties. I was asked to give a few words of testimony before I went under, and I assured everyone in a shrill voice that Jesus was indeed my Savior. Then in the name of the Father, the Son, and the Holy Ghost I was bent backwards under the water.

I held my nose and did not panic, as instructed, but in that moment I may have remembered a time before I had learned to swim when I had impulsively thrown myself into a small plastic boat floating on the deep end of a neighbor's pool in California. The boat capsized on top of me, and I struggled underneath it for what felt like a long while. Then suddenly my mother was there, under the water beside me, and grabbing my hand. She brought me forcibly to the surface and pushed me onto the concrete deck. Which was not bad at all for a woman still recovering from the paralysis of polio. For many months she had lain immobile on her bed. But she had been rescued from that disease. And for my mother to rescue me from under the water—that is what it meant to be saved. And when Dr. Bowser lifted me, dripping and snorting, back up to the surface, I was saved once more.

So that should have been the end of it—of my being saved. I had invited Jesus into my heart, made a public profession of faith, and been baptized. I was free to pick up bulletins and wait for any further call, should God decide to speak to me as he did to Samuel in the night.

The funny thing is, some part of God did speak to me—or at least come to me. It happened in broad daylight, and quite outside the protocol set up for him in our orderly church, though he came to me after the morning service one day in the emptiness of that sanctuary. It wasn't exactly a tree full of angels, as William Blake reported seeing as a boy. But, in the words of our old-time song, a song the mystics themselves could sing, it was good enough for me.

I was nine years old, and we were at worship on a sundrenched Sunday morning in late spring or early summer. Once again, what Dr. Bowser preached about I cannot now resurrect, but something that he said must have stirred a longing in me. After the benediction, the congregation emptied onto the front steps in the sunshine, and I remained in the dim shade of the sanctuary. I was restless, I remember that. Hungry for something. Just what, I didn't know.

Once, on Easter, I had come to church with my pockets full of foil-wrapped chocolate eggs. We had gone on a hunt with Easter baskets that morning, and my mother had made us promise not to eat anything we had found until after church. A Pharisee in my younger years, I interpreted "after church" to mean anytime after the choir sang its final multilayered amen, and I came prepared to partake of my spoils. During the long sermon my hands trembled at the edge of my pockets. Then the permitted moment came, and both hands plunged in, only to immerse themselves in two leaking holsters of chocolate, warm and wet. That was an epiphany all its own.

But just now I didn't want any chocolate. I wanted—something else. I began to wander the tiered maze of Sunday school rooms and fellowship halls at the back of our church. (Dante, I now think, had nothing on us when it came to labyrinthine architecture of sacred space.) I wandered and began to pray, over and over, for something from God. The prayer became obsessive and repetitive, more and more urgent within me. And still I wandered. And still I prayed—desperate, it seemed. Finally I climbed four flights of wooden steps—from the basement to the top floor—crossed a small, cloistered room, and opened a narrow door onto the balcony of the sanctuary.

That is when my inarticulate prayer was granted. In that moment of coming through the door I walked into a presence that had been there, I was quite sure, all along. It was quiet, powerful, good, and deep. It was a presence that included me, and all things around me. The clock at the back of the sanctuary, the miserably worn rug in the aisle, the chipped wooden balcony seats, the faded red curtains behind them—all things were permeated by whatever this quiet, ongoing presence was. They were not different, but more themselves, more what they had been all along, richly sustained, transfigured in their everyday best. I had not come to a different place but was seeing the place as it always was. Every minute of perception up to this point had just been bumping about in the dark.

I drifted down the main stairs, out the doors at the front of the church, and into brilliant sunshine. The walnut tree by the curb struck me with dumb wonder, so immeasurably green, so rightly itself. Likewise the blue sky burned with an intensity unknown but gloriously ordinary. And the people, all of the lovely people, milling about, talking, waving. How blessed they were. How blessed I was to be among them. There in their midst I saw my father. He was speaking to someone, not looking at me, but in that moment I knew what it was to simply and deeply cherish him. *This is my father*, I said to myself, and I knew he loved me deeply as well, more deeply than I would ever fathom—though in that moment I seemed to be fathoming more than I ever had.

So that was pretty much it. That was how some part of God came to me, and how my heart was strangely warmed. In later years I learned some words with which to label my experience: *ecstasy, epiphany, mystical communion.* In Julian of Norwich it is the *all well* in "all shall be well and all shall be well and all manner of thing shall be well." In Wordsworth it is the "sense sublime / Of something far more deeply interfused." In Henry Vaughan, "Bright shoots of everlastingness." But the only words I knew at the time were not allowed at Victory Bible: the baptism of the Holy Spirit. I knew about the baptism of the Holy Spirit from reading a popular book of that time, *The Cross and the Switchblade*, by David Wilkerson. Wilkerson was a Pentecostal minister who converted gang members in New York City. They accepted Christ and then, after an anguished period of praying and desiring, the Holy Spirit came to them and they spoke in tongues. Speaking in tongues was anathema to my Victory Bible Sunday school teachers, who emphasized to us again and again that when you received Christ, you were also given the Holy Spirit at that very moment, as part of the bargain, whether you felt anything or not. We were trained to respect fact, not feeling.

I hadn't spoken in tongues or anything. Far from it. In fact, I had not uttered a word while under the influence of whatever it was I was under the influence of. But the reality of this divine presence I could not doubt. And the uniqueness of the experience I could not doubt. And the experience of the experience I could not deny to myself. But because my experience didn't fit what had been prescribed for me, I didn't tell anyone about it. Not even my mother, who saved me. Not even my father, who wiped me clean and loved me with love immeasurable. The only person I told was my great-grandfather, an old-time Pentecostal preacher in Oklahoma City. And he was dead. But I figured he would understand and maybe even approve of what had happened to me. I loved to look at one particular photograph we had of him—as solemn, stern, and white-bearded as Robert E. Lee, the most unlikely candidate for ecstatic communion with the Spirit. As are we all, I suppose.

I remember keeping another secret of this sort from my parents, and I wonder now if it might have been as spiritually sensitive to me as my later epiphany in the church. When I first learned to read, at age six, I found on a shelf of our rented home a book by the name of *The Lion, the Witch, and the Wardrobe,* by C. S. Lewis. I had never read a story of this length before, but the pictures looked promising, and for two weeks I labored through it. The reading may have been difficult, but it soon turned into a labor of love. Lucy, Tumnus, the White Witch, the Beavers, Aslan, Cair Paravel—I was swept into another world of grave and sparkling delight. When I finished the book I said to myself I could think of no better thing in life than to write a story just like this. In other words, I could think of nothing better than to go back to Narnia on my own terms, through my own wardrobe. For the time being, however, what I had read was much too precious to talk about, to profane by trying to communicate in spoken words. If I talked about it, Narnia might go away. When the fairies bring you gold, it is a secret you must keep.

In his book *The Most Reluctant Convert: C. S. Lewis's Journey to Faith,* my friend David Downing says the conversion of C. S. Lewis himself occurred in at least three stages. The first and by far the earliest stage was what Lewis called the baptism of his imagination. In his case it came through reading many different works of literature, but primarily through the fantasy of George MacDonald. MacDonald's stories, particularly the novel *Phantastes,* filled Lewis with a longing for the good and for the infinite. This tale he read as a teenager, and reread many times thereafter. Then, as a young professor, after a long intellectual struggle, he kneeled in his room and gave his assent to God, to theism. His final conversion, specifically to Christianity, was more mysterious and spontaneous. Two years later he was riding to the Whipsnade Zoo in Oxford in the sidecar of his brother Warren's motorcycle.

Without quite knowing why, without really intending to, he gave himself to the presence of Christ and returned home a changed man. In medieval manner, Downing labels these three stages as conversions of the imagination, the intellect, and the will.

I wonder now if I have not undergone a somewhat similar process, though it sounds silly to assign such categories to the spiritual experience of such young years. At age six my imagination was perhaps baptized by Narnia, and thereafter by John Bunyan. At age seven I gave what passed for intellectual assent in a prayer in my room. And at age nine it seems my will was overtaken by the palpable presence of God. First there is a felt possibility of faith, then a conscious desire for faith, and then at some point, in its own time, an experiential fulfillment of faith.

Or am I just falling into my old and regrettable churchified habit of turning a mystery into a paradigm? God knows. For even Lewis's steps of conversion are not as simple and discrete as I have made them out to be. A few months before his prayer of intellectual assent, Lewis had an experience on a bus in which a "door to belief" somehow seemed to open for him. And in the last months of his life, while sick in bed, he seems to have had an ecstatic vision of the divine. "Oh," he sighed afterward, "I never imagined. I never imagined." All that can be said, I suppose, is that God meets us at many times and in many ways, ways that exceed even our richest imaginations. And God knows I have made the foolish mistake before of trying to pattern myself after C. S. Lewis, particularly in my earliest years as a college teacher. It was a great relief to conclude that he was smarter than I was, and to go on my more pedestrian but no-less-wonderful way.

And yet, I think Lewis would approve of what I might call a second baptism of my imagination. This happened in graduate school when I first read Edmund Spenser's *Faerie Queene*. (As for my great-grandfather, I think this might have confused him greatly.) There was something about the quality of Spenser's sixteenth-century verse, the quiet contentment that gently pervades the world of the Redcrosse Knight and of Una, Florimell, Amoret, and Calidore—a something that brought me sweetly back as nothing ever had before to a dim noonday balcony in an old church in Oregon. How could it be that Spenser knew? How could it be that a poet who wrote four hundred years in the past seemed to know exactly what had happened to me, seemed to know the same deep, solemn pleasure I had been found by and still hoped to find again? The writer of the New Testament book of Hebrews is quite sure that we are surrounded in our journey by "a cloud of witnesses," and it seemed to me that Edmund Spenser was one of them. It seems to me now that some parts of literature are nothing more and nothing less than the active communion of the saints. When I first finished *The Faerie Queene* and got to Spenser's earnest entreaty for Sabbath rest, I cried for a long time. I cried because I still believed there was a Jesus, and he had come to comfort me.

Care to Dance?

I KNEW THAT DANCING was wrong. When Miss Waring played the scratchy phonograph on the gym stage and girls rushed for the sweaty hands of little boys to begin the simplest of folk reels, I would solemnly mount the stage steps and deliver a carefully handwritten note: "Please excuse Paul from all dancing in Physical Education class. For religious reasons, we feel it would be best if he did not participate." Without undoing her lipstick smile, Miss Waring would send me to the luxury of a silent classroom. There I would page through three entire battles of the Civil War before my classmates returned, their faces unusually flushed and healthy for all the evil they had done.

One Saturday morning, over ordinarily peaceful pancakes, my parents found that my older brother had gone to a dance on Friday night. Words grew hot as pancakes grew cold. "But what's wrong with it?" he wailed.

"Son, dancing is suggestive, erotic, indecent, and unseemly. It's dark at a dance, and there is usually drinking going on. We should not be associated with that type of activity." My father said this sternly, conscious he was erecting a moral roadblock of insurmountable proportions.

My mother's face was red and her hands trembled. "Oh, oh, oh, Davey," she flustered out. "We just don't do that sort of thing. It's not the place for a Christian to maintain his witness."

Davey sighed, sputtered, and jerked. He knew he could not win.

But neither could my parents. They must have expended their censoring energies upon my brother, for three years later, in June of ninth grade, I was quietly allowed to go to a dance myself. Not that I actually intended to participate. No, it was merely time I inspected this evil firsthand.

The school cafeteria was dark—they were right about that. Ultraviolet lights were glowing on a melee surrounded by onlookers in chairs. George Palmquist and a friend of his sat staring at the floor, quietly drunk—my parents were right about that, too. On a stage above the dancers was a local band making great amounts of music. I glimpsed one band member slightly offstage, embracing the shadow of a girl. Unseemly.

I sat with my friend Vince Wilson, Baptist bred and new to the darkness. Together we studied the dancers. At last I said, "It doesn't look that hard, you know." Vince did not reply. So I turned to Leanne Akers (who was a backslidden Baptist, but still very nice), and I asked if she would show me how.

"Certainly," she said, and whisked me away.

Under the ultraviolet lights, her white dress gave off an unearthly purplish glow. My blue shirt and white tie burned with the same intensity. I had seen this kind of thing in mineral exhibits and tropical aquariums, but now Leanne Akers and I shone like the rocks and the fish. It was splendid. King David never had it so good, cavorting in broad daylight before the ark of the covenant.

We found a spot on the floor relatively free of circling elbows and shimmering hips. My second-grade sweetheart, Vivian Starr, appeared nearby, tilting her neck and making delicate swimming motions with her arms. She looked at the ceiling with her eyes half-closed and rocked her forehead back and forth. She might have been ecstatic, she might have been bored—I could not tell. Across from me, Leanne Akers began to chug her arms and rotate her body in the manner of a top-loading washing machine.

It was obviously time to exhibit my stuff. Cleverly, I swung my arms back and forth, feinted one foot forward and quickly retracted it. Then I lashed out with the other foot and retrieved it as well. All very provocative. I swung my arms at the conservative pace of a mile run and kept on feinting my feet in remarkable syncopation.

When the music stopped, I returned to Vince Wilson on the sidelines. "Nothing to it, really," I told him. "How did I look?"

"How did you look?" he said. I did not like the incredulity in his voice. "You just sorta dabbled your feet in front of you like you were doing the hokey-pokey."

Not so, I thought. Well, maybe so, I thought. Perhaps I could use more practice.

Leanne Akers obliged again, then Heather Hobbs. That was my third dance, and Heather Hobbs only tepidly swung her wrists and padded her feet in vaguely different directions. She obviously needed a lesson or two in gusto and body language;

this was no time to be demure. And there to my left was Archie Corliss, dressed in a suit of all things, and dancing the way you would march in a band.

And so it went. Except for the slow dances, which looked alarmingly intimate, I took the floor at every turn, exercising my *noblesse oblige* toward even the most unpopular girls. Their braces glittered gratefully, and I felt the pleasure known only to the generous of heart.

But somewhere along the eighth or ninth dance, swinging my arms and feinting my feet, something changed. At first it was just a sliver of boredom that entered my mind. But it soon festered. Deep down, I thought I knew why: there were limits to my repertoire of response to the music, and I had reached them. Like Jaques in *As You Like It,* I was not one for dancing measures. I wanted to ask Leanne Akers her feelings on this matter, but the band was too loud—I could only watch her agitate on full-wash cycle. I wanted to ask her why it was we were glowing in the dark out here, a human half-acre of Mexican jumping beans.

Was it my parental conscience, returning to haunt me? Perhaps, but perhaps not. Because now I was thinking of the Junior Classics hardback edition of *Gulliver's Travels* that lay half-read in my bedroom, of the fresh morning trail that led through the ferns to McDonald Forest, of the smell of Mrs. Coleman's lawn that I would mow the next day. The ultraviolet churn began to pale before these prospects, and all of a sudden, dancing was not evil, just dull.

I was astounded, elated even. It was not a moral choice after all. The world was a different place than I had ever thought it—a good place, on the whole, and I would choose the best parts, and conscience would not equally matter for every choosing. Or maybe conscience did matter, and the most important moral choice was to separate strong pleasure from weak, the good from the banal. The trick was to enjoy something a long time—maybe forever.

I staggered off the dance floor, laden with surprise, and again took my seat beside watchful Vince Wilson. "Is it fun?" he asked.

Certainly, I thought to myself, it had been pleasurable for a season. I looked at my friend from the distant side of raw experience. "You ought to try it," I told him.

All the World

AFTER SUPPER WE GATHERED for an evening devotional, sitting more or mostly less together on a grassy slope above the water. The sun had not quite touched the forest and held the lake in a glitter of wavelets, green and gold. The snowbank across from us had been fractured off by some daring footwork, and bits of bergs now floated in wreckage. At the end of the lake, the far end, a thin smudge of smoke and a tinkle of pots marked the campsite of another group, newly arrived. Occasionally a figure would glide from a small stand of fir to the edge of the lake and back again. We had no idea who they were.

I was sitting far from Jennifer Smith, whom I admired, but very close to Roy Percy, our youth group *sponsor*, as we called him, who was leaning against a silvered snag with Bible in hand. While he searched for a likely passage, I plucked at a white plume of beargrass beside me, crushing each flowerlet until my fingers oozed with the scent.

"Okay, gang," Roy Percy said in an official sort of way. He had found the right verse. "Listen up."

A dirt clod exploded at Jennifer's feet, and several boys laughed. This, I had noticed, was Alex Harmon's method of courtship. According to my mother, Alex Harmon was slightly retarded, something I was never supposed to mention to others.

"Listen up," Roy Percy said again, and a restless calm descended upon us. "I'd just like to share with you something that the Lord has been laying on my heart." Roy Percy had assumed a carefully modulated tone, borrowed perhaps from his missionary father. I had once seen a picture of his father in swim trunks, chest thrust out. He stood knee-deep in Lake Michigan and held a one-year-old version of Roy Percy in a single outstretched hand, as if ready to juggle. Of course, this was the same Roy Percy who went on to climb Mt. Kilimanjaro as a mere boy. I knew because he often told me.

"Here we've been out in God's country this weekend, enjoying the fantastic beauty of his creation all around us. And yet—" Here Roy Percy slapped his forearm. So did I. Mosquitoes had come to dwell with us in the cool of the evening. "And yet, what the Lord has been reminding me is that it is not enough to just enjoy his creation. God tells us in his Word that we must testify to all people of Christ's saving work on the cross. God not only made the world for us to enjoy. He also sent his only Son to die for us."

Now everyone was slapping mosquitoes. Slap. Slap. Close enough together to sound like a desultory applause.

"Have you ever stopped to consider how many of your friends do not know Jesus as their Savior? Have you ever stopped to think how many of them are going to hell because we are too busy enjoying ourselves—or too afraid to bear witness to them? The apostle Paul could say he was not ashamed of the gospel of Christ. Can you? Do you hide your light under a bushel because you are afraid of ridicule and persecution?"

There were whisperings behind me, requests for bug repellent. A new splendor of sun shone on the snowy side of the lake, the side we had come to in the morning. We were lost, then, twenty redeemed high-school youth from the Victory Bible Church of Marysville, Oregon. According to the map, George Lake was one simple mile from the trail. And according to the United States Forest Service on the back of the map, "Cross-country travel in the Mt. Washington Wilderness Area of Central Oregon is relatively easy, due to the open nature of forests growing in dry volcanic soils." I was relatively sure I could get us here, and Roy Percy was relatively generous enough to let me try. And fail.

So where the trail dipped down to the lava fields of Belknap Crater I struck out cross country, my peers in tow, lakeward bound up steep open forest. After the requisite short mile, I began to notice how extraordinarily silent my church friends had become. No extemporaneous choruses of "Do Lord," no gales of laughter at branches unleashed in unsuspecting faces, no questions about the subspecies of lupine underfoot, no questions, even, of how much further we had to go. Merely dogged, sullen, labored breathing, and the occasional sweaty stare.

I had slowed to the prudent rest step recommended by Harvey Manning in the second edition of *The Freedom of the Hills,* locking the knee of my downhill leg before shifting my weight higher. Even so, the parade of backpacks lengthened behind me, tottering on listless legs like orange-red-lavender clowns on stilts. So I turned and gestured feebly to the right, this to improve morale by announcing my intent of contouring the hill instead of climbing it straight on. Also, the lake might actually be to the right of us. But Roy Percy would not be fooled.

"Why go right?" he asked, puffing up to my side. There were melon-shaped sweat stains under the arms of his chambray shirt. He crooked his pudgy thumbs beneath the straps of his bureau-sized Kelty and made his voice loud enough for everyone to hear. "It's got to be up and left, through those trees." What he meant to say was, "You are lost, and I am not. Ha, ha, ha."

I shrugged and headed off a little less to the right than I had planned, but still kept my course, not his. Roy Percy made no pretense of pursuing me and went his way. Our followers clumped at the fork of two imaginary roads, paused to consider, and with one accord made mine the one less traveled by. Nevertheless, I kept as far to the right as I could without losing sight of the others. If the lake should appear in my direction and not in theirs—a glimmer of water through shrouds of lichen that hung from the trees—how sweet that would be.

"Here it is!" called Roy Percy. His voice carried a gloating echo from over the brow of the hill. He had found the lake not somehow, but triumphantly. When I reached him, he was resting one foot on a shattered stump as if atop the conquered summit of Kilimanjaro. He gestured over his shoulder with his thumb. "Hey, right here, pal. Just took a little route finding, that's all." I did not like the way Roy Percy took credit for his luck. We're all lost, I thought, but if you happen to get there, that's called leadership.

The lake was shaded partway around by hemlock forest, from which we emerged on snowbanks overarching the water. The far shore rose in bright sandy meadows of lupine and beargrass to the cockeyed plug of Mt. Washington, overlooking the supine lake in dark phallic splendor. We made camp on the sunny side, and nearly everyone changed into swimsuits after lunch.

I, however, asked Roy Percy if I could leave to climb Belknap Crater. This would mean retracing our steps to the Pacific Crest Trail, threading the lava flow, kicking up hot scree to the summit, and returning by supper. I really did want to climb the crater—it would increase my collection of visited summits—but I also wanted to show Roy Percy I could find George Lake myself, albeit on the second try. Roy Percy said I could go.

Belknap was a parched place. From the top, I held out my arms over miles of lava, huge blocks and chunks and boot-shredding shards of it, blank as the moon, a thirsty land. I could have backflipped into the crater behind me, a hollow stadium filled with snow. Instead I turned and more conventionally leapt inside and glissaded down on the edges of my boots, sending sprays of ice up into my face. At the very bottom I let the ice weep onto my chest. I saw the walls of snow rise around me. I saw the rim of the summit circle my head. I saw the blue bowl of sky empty itself. I saw the sun pulse white. Nature seemed void of all things save my somewhat curious self. I entertained the thought of volcano vents open beneath me, covered over with a thin crust of snow. One misstep and down I would plunge into cool darkness, falling, falling to the dead molten fires. How surprising it would be, how new, how welcome, to float unharmed in soothing shade to the Center of the Earth—to Hades or even Sheol, perhaps.

Once there, I would dust myself off and, making wise use of the Ten Essentials in my rucksack (which included compass, matches, and candle stubs), I would carefully climb through chambers and passageways to a hidden cave entrance at George Lake, where I would nonchalantly walk into the sunlight—filthy, hungry, a bit bruised—to find Jennifer Smith in the same red bikini I had seen her in just after lunch. Victory Bible girls did not normally wear bikinis, red or otherwise, and I had seen very few in my sixteen years. Jennifer Smith, however, had just moved north from California and knew no better. When I issued from the cave she would run up shyly and touch my arm and ask how I had ever managed to find my way to George Lake from the Center of the Earth. I would laugh pleasantly, lay a rock-grimed hand on her soft round shoulder, and say, "Just took a little route finding, that's all."

Roy Percy reopened his Bible and brushed a mosquito from the sweat of his brow. "Here in Matthew, Jesus says, 'Whosoever therefore shall confess me before men, him will I confess also before my Father which is in heaven. But whosoever shall deny me before men, him will I also deny before my Father which is in heaven.' Do you realize what Jesus is saying? What Jesus is saying to us in this passage is that if we don't tell other people about him we aren't really Christians after all. Jesus will condemn us before the Father in heaven. On the last day we will say to him, 'Lord, Lord,' but he will reply, 'I never knew you: depart from me, ye evildoers.' And we'll go to spend our eternity in hell. In hell, gang, the same as the people we refused to share our faith with in the first place."

The whispering behind me had ceased. I had stopped plucking at the beargrass plume and was now squeezing the stalk in my fist.

Roy Percy paused, then turned and pointed with outstretched arm to the hidden campsite at the uttermost end of the lake. He held this pose for several seconds—a modern, beefy, male version of the bronze statue of Sacajawea at the state capitol that pointed the way for the bronze statues of Lewis and Clark.

"How many of us," he asked, "have the courage and compassion to go to our neighbors at this very lake and share the gospel with them? How many of us love Jesus enough to let our testimony be known—even to strangers? I'd like to leave all of you with this challenge. Here we are, with the good news of eternal life. And there they are, in need of that good news. The question is, what are we going to do about it? It's a question each of you should be asking yourselves right now.

"Jesus has commanded us as his disciples to preach the gospel to every creature. The question is, are we actually willing to be his disciples? Men on the mission field cross the ocean and give their lives for the sake of the gospel. Is it so much to ask to cross one small lake and give twenty short minutes of your time to share your personal testimony?" He gave a little chuckle to let us know it was not too much to ask. "Think about it, gang," he said.

I did, grinding my heels into the soil as if searching for a secure foundation. My plume of beargrass was by now destroyed.

"Let's pray," said Roy Percy. "Dear Lord, we just pray, Lord, that, Lord, you would give us the courage to stand up and be counted for you. Keep us from being the sort of lukewarm Christians, Lord, that you have said in your Word that you will spew out of your mouth. And we just pray, Lord, that you will embolden our hearts to point the way for those who are lost. We pray these things in the name of Jesus, Amen."

I opened my eyes, which I had closed during the prayer, and saw a profound silence in search of transition. I saw it in our faces—a desperate collective impulse to find a way back to the safety of the profane world. At last, in our lengthening moment of need, a precious dirt clod exploded among us. We praised it inwardly, giving thanks for the sweet showering of real earth and for the hands that had prepared it. Another dirt clod burst in the lupine, and this time a few of us laughed nervously. The third one hit Jennifer Smith square in the lap. "Stop it, you guys!" she squealed softly, and then everyone laughed, even Roy Percy.

"Let's throw her in the lake!" said Alex Harmon.

"Yeah!" said the other boys.

Jennifer Smith ran up the grassy slope to camp, and the boys ran after her. The girls ran after the boys to protect Jennifer Smith. Which left me, alone, with Roy Percy.

We stood up slowly and yawned and stretched more than was necessary. I felt him about to say something to me, something like, "Well, big guy, I guess it's time you and me headed down to the other end of the lake to share the good news." And I would have to go—the Great Commission could not be laughed off with a few dirt clods. I would have to introduce myself to a group of strangers and convince them to be lost and found in the time that it took them to boil their water for some Mountain House freeze-dried shrimp Creole. With Roy Percy, no less. A wilderness version of the dreaded door-to-door evangelism.

Two years before, in the ninth grade, I had actually witnessed door to door for an entire weekend. It was part of an evangelism explosion that was to turn our neighborhood upside down for Jesus Christ. I went with another boy my age, just as the disciples had been sent out in pairs; we took turns. Our approach was carefully indirect. When the unsuspecting occupants cracked their door, we would first say, clipboards in hand, that we were taking a survey. We asked if they went to church, if they believed in God, things like that. Then we asked if they had heard of the Four Spiritual

Laws. Since very few people had, we were virtually assured of the chance to pull from hiding a small yellow pamphlet which explained just what these Four Spiritual Laws were. The first one was that God loved you and had a wonderful plan for your life. I remembered this one best because very often we would not get to the second one. If by chance we were able to get to the fourth spiritual law, however, we could then pop the question: would they like to receive Christ as their personal Savior by praying the prayer printed in the pamphlet? At this point, according to the training movie we had watched, the person would probably have invited you into her living room. You would be sitting next to her on her couch. She would say yes and you would hold her hand while she tearfully prayed the printed prayer aloud. Then you were done and could walk away with a notch on your belt, a definite soul-winner.

On my weekend, however, I got past the fourth spiritual law only once. Conditions weren't the best, since the woman had not yet invited us in—she stood half-hidden by the door in her bathrobe. In spite of sharp eyes and graying hair, she looked fairly young.

"Would you like to receive Jesus Christ as your personal Savior by praying this prayer?" I asked, holding the pamphlet where she could see the proper words.

"Yes," she nodded.

"You would?" I was quite stunned. "Here's the prayer, then, right here." I pointed it out with my finger. "It starts out—"

"Shut up," said the woman. "I'm praying it."

This struck me as a rude thing for a person to say at the moment of her conversion. Also, I needed to tell her it wouldn't count unless she said the prayer aloud, preferably sitting next to me on the couch in her living room.

"Okay," she said, "I'm through." She shut the door without even bothering to keep her copy of the Four Spiritual Laws. My partner and I agreed that she had not left much time for what the movie called follow-up evangelism.

So I stood there alone with Roy Percy, ready to do it all over again. Only this time there would not be the well-defined comforts of porch steps and doorbells. People expect strangers at their front door from time to time, but I had an idea they went camping to be alone. Especially if they had taken the trouble to find a wilderness lake off the trail. Maybe I could tell Roy Percy that I wasn't sure we'd be able to find our way back in the dark. The sun was in the forest now, and we stood in shade.

Roy Percy slapped his arm and inspected the remains of a blood-gorged mosquito. "Got the little sucker," he said, and chuckled without quite catching my eye. Then he too went up to camp. Just like that. As if there were nothing else in particular he had in mind to do. I waited to see if he had just gone to get his jacket or bug juice. But Roy Percy did not return.

I wandered to the edge of the lake, now calm in the wake of the afternoon breeze that had ceased with the day. I stood with my toes almost in the water and watched the shady rim of darkness overtake the surface. Then I turned and watched the sun sink deeper into the hemlocks, outlining their crooked tops in a greenish glow.

I thought for some reason of my Aunt Lillian, whom I saw just every five years or so on her missionary furlough. I thought of her kind voice and her listening eyes, of the way that I was always glad when she sat beside me on the couch. I had seen her once, early in the morning, sitting on the floor in a corner and praying with her hands flat over her face. She was not married and spoke of the Lord Jesus as if she loved him more than any other man. I wondered if Aunt Lillian went door to door in the Japanese fishing village where she lived and shared the Four Spiritual Laws in Japanese. If she did, the Japanese fishermen probably invited her inside right away, where they would sit, not on a couch, but on straw mats, perhaps. Everyone would want to pray the translated prayer with her. For Aunt Lillian it would come quite naturally.

But I wondered what she would do right now if she were here. Would Aunt Lillian stroll to the campsite at the end of the lake, invite herself in on a chocolate-pudding dessert, and speak, quite naturally, in between spoonfuls, of her constant love for the Lord Jesus? I didn't know.

I fixed my eyes on the clump of firs, small churchlike spires, that marked the unknown camp. They were less distinct now, dusky in the gathering shade that had crossed the lake. *Who will go for us?* I thought. *How beautiful upon the mountains are the feet of him that bringeth good tidings.* How beautiful. How beautiful. In the dim distance a single figure slipped from the trees to the shore of the lake opposite me. A human being, in the image of God, who perchance did not know Jesus. The thought held a precarious and unlawful delight. I watched the figure sit down on the shore and saw a flash of silver—supper pots to be cleaned, perhaps, or a rainbow trout slapping the surface nearby. I wondered if she saw me. *She,* for I thought of the person as female and feminine, a secular version of Aunt Lillian, a wilderness version of the woman in the bathrobe, a grown-up version of Jennifer Smith. I wondered what she would say to me if she could speak across the water, what

Macedonian vision she would send in my dreams. The bit of silver flashed again. This time I clearly saw it was in her hands.

In the same moment the music began. First a high, thin, cautious note, quivering like a bird just learning to fly. Then another, more firm, and a liquid series, dipping like swallows on the surface of the lake by some wonderful plan. The woman was playing a flute, I decided. I sat to listen, knees against my chest. What siren song or hymn of praise it was I did not know. But the sound was at home here. The breath-blown notes became themselves in the lake and the trees and the lava-rich air, and called all of these, the fullness of the place, into sharper being.

I uncurled my legs till my feet felt the water, clean and cold, slip into my shoes with a purifying ache. After a while, in the deepening twilight, I could no longer see the flute or its player. So I slowly lay down, resting my head in a fountain of beargrass. My head was dry and my feet were wet. I was both. I watched the plume at my head reach into the sky, into darkening blue, as the flute played on, now wavering, now clear, enduing the silence between each breath with new perfection. In the flowerlets I saw the hard sweet shine of the evening star, held by music from the dawn of creation. It occurred to me that the music was for Roy Percy too. Was he listening? Could he hear?

When the cold was too much, I drew my feet out of the lake and stripped off my shoes and socks. My shriveled toes were utterly numb, but as I pressed them into the pumice shore they throbbed like the stars in a dying fall.

THE MOUNTAIN

Lead thou me
to the rock that is higher than I . . .

—Psalm 61:2

Where Are the Leaders of Tomorrow?

SOMETIMES, WHEN I THINK about my years as a student at Wheaton College, that evangelical Vatican of the Midwest, I remember Wordsworth's thoughts in *The Prelude* about his days at Cambridge University. The poet who loved the mountains of the Lake District so long and so well could only look back on his time in the foreign fields of East Anglia and say, "I was not for that hour, / Nor for that place." I wasn't from the Lake District, I was from Oregon. But I loved the Cascade Range in much the way that Wordsworth loved his own green hills, and I couldn't see much use in a satisfied suburb in a dull, flat country. There weren't too many trails to hike, and people were always going *shopping,* as they say it so quaintly in Chicago.

Unlike Wordsworth, perhaps, I made my dissatisfactions known. I wasn't some loser from Illinois, I told anyone who cared to listen—I was a climber guy from the Northwest. I rappelled out my fourth-story dorm window every decent chance I got, and climbed up and down the elevator shaft at night. I scaled a women's dorm, the science building. Even the old cottonwood trees on front campus. Soon I had earned a name, and when Major Winslow demanded it the day I showed up for ROTC in red, white, and blue boxer shorts, I told him it was Cliff Hanger. That cost me several demerits for "giving false name to superior," not to mention "disrespect to uniform," but it was the name I wanted, the name I had.

Sometime during my first year, Mark Hatfield was disinvited to speak in chapel. I took this rather personally. Hatfield was a senator from the State of Oregon. When I was in the fifth grade, Mark Hatfield was our governor. Mark O. Hatfield, to be precise. I knew because my class had made a field trip to his office in the capitol, and we were each given a letter with his signature. The name was printed out for us at the very bottom, but the signature was a series of squiggles that flatlined like a fatality. Which he apparently was, as far as our college president, Hudson Armerding, was concerned. Armerding was the one who disinvited Hatfield, even though the entire faculty begged to differ. He would never say why, though most people thought it was because of Hatfield's opposition to the war in Vietnam. The president was very proud of his own time in the Navy, and I think it was because of him that we still had mandatory ROTC in 1973. I also knew that Armerding went on lots of trips to Texas to raise funds for the college. Our Texas supporters were not a very dovish lot.

A few of us thought to stage a protest, only to find that according to the revised rules in the student handbook, demonstrations could not be held inside of, in front of, or across the street from any college structure. Meaning: no protests on campus. These new rules were a legacy of the late sixties, when demonstrations evidently had occurred on campus. We, the students of the seventies, were very often complimented for our relative quiescence. We didn't know whether to be proud or ashamed of this. Our older siblings rolled their eyes, but our chapel speakers praised us for being "Wheaton's kind of students"—the kind shown in recruiting ads for the college, invariably pictured as a well-dressed young man sitting erect at a tidy desk.

So instead of staging a protest we held a little prayer meeting on the day that Hatfield did not speak. We offered our miserable, whiny prayers in the basement of the old chapel across the street from the new one. We were so pained, so sincere, so restrained in our efforts. It made me sick to pretend to be so longsuffering. "Dear Lord," we said, "we just pray that your truth would shine in the hearts of those entrusted with the power to make decisions on our campus, and that they would see your light. We trust your sovereign guidance in this disappointing situation, and *bublah, bublah, bublah.*" If you have been in the evangelical subculture long enough, you can say these kinds of things in your sleep.

And then there were The Boys. The Boys were a group of senior jocks who lived in a house off campus. They were not particularly nice, especially to the freshman jocks. So these freshmen raided their house one night and made off with some prized items. Then the next night they asked Cliff Hanger to help them to display these items in prominent places. The tropical helmet we stuck on top of the flagpole. The letterman's jacket ended up on the cornice of the new chapel. And a yellow diamond highway sign was seen next morning dangling across from the library, eighty feet up in a cottonwood.

The Boys never figured out who had heisted their stuff. But thanks to my cherished reputation, they found out who had hoisted it. The Sunday afternoon before final exams, I was reading my Bible in my room when one of The Boys walked in. He sat in a chair uninvited and leveled me with a long stare.

"The Boys know what you done," he said, and planted a very big pause. "You're wanted at The Boys' house at seven o'clock tonight."

"Thanks for the invitation," I said uncertainly. "Are you serving refreshments?"

"No funny business," he said. "Be there at seven o'clock."

"Can you tell me where it is, exactly?"

He looked at me with pained contempt. "Everyone knows where The Boys live," he said with drama. Then he gave me another stare and walked out.

I knew what The Boys had been up to lately. Two weeks ago they had broken the arm of a campus cop. One week ago they had summoned a guy from a neighboring dorm, and when he showed up, they stripped him naked and spray-painted his body green. So I cleared out of my room that night, well before seven o'clock, and spent the rest of finals week with a friend in another dorm. That summer The Boys went on a road trip to Oregon and threatened my father with legal action. Years later, one of them had a short career as a head coach in the NBA. Everyone said what a swell guy he was, and what a shame that he got fired.

By the time I got to be a senior, I lived in an off-campus house myself. I sublet a room from a climber friend and his new wife, recent graduates of the college. In their basement they ran the U-Neek Food Co-op, which consisted of three usually broken refrigerators they kept stocked from their nightly rounds of dumpster diving behind the local grocery stores. Once, in March, we found seven huge heart-shaped boxes of Valentine's chocolates, still wrapped in cellophane. I sent three of them to some very deserving girls on campus and saved the rest for a climbing trip to Colorado.

My roommate for that year in the house was an eighteen-year-old senior on the debate team—like many at Wheaton, a driven child prodigy. His parents had firm plans for him to attend law school and threw a fit when he decided to go into the Peace Corps instead. Halfway through the year, they told him to move out of the house because of my bad influence. I was offended. "It's not a Bill Gothard world," I told him. "Your parents can't make all the decisions. Especially these kind." He listened intently and wrote a letter to his folks, telling them his determination to remain in the house, under my deplorable influence.

On graduation weekend, we hosted a party at the house for our friends and their families. They crowded in and chattered brightly about our prospects. It was a lovely spring afternoon. At some point I found myself on our back porch, looking out at the weedy lawn with the father of a brilliant young woman who did not much like to climb. He was the director of a Bible camp and conference center on the New Jersey shore, and just now he looked distressed. For a while he said nothing at all. Then he burst out, pounding his fist on the porch railing as if he were shouting from a pulpit, "Where are the leaders of tomorrow?"

I realized immediately the question was rhetorical, that I wasn't being personally addressed at all. Only publicly accused. The answer to the question was that tomorrow's evangelical leaders were not to be found inside this house. We had gone untrained. The ship was sinking, and the younger generation was lounging poolside with martinis.

During baccalaureate, the graduates sat on risers on the ample platform of the chapel and sang together, a cappella, "May the Mind of Christ My Savior." It is for me a sweet and moving song to this day. President Armerding, seated in front of us, got up out of his chair and, while we were singing, looked each of us in the eye, one by one, nodding his head. He was commissioning us. I liked that. In that moment, I liked him.

I remembered a time the previous year when, desperate to transfer out, I had paced the streets feverishly, trying to decide what to do. After several weeks of turmoil, I sat in the bushes against the wall of the library and just cried. Real hard. When I finished crying, I knew I would stay. And I knew, in a strange way, that I didn't have to work so hard to be Cliff Hanger anymore. That I could just be me. A somewhat new me. That I could be for this hour and for this place in some temporary sense, and that Oregon would be there when I got back. I felt very certain of this. It was as if God had spoken to me. And perhaps he did.

But I still have to come to terms with the strangeness of my college experience. We were supposedly the best and the brightest, the hope of the future for the subculture. Not for the gospel but for the subculture, a subculture in which war protesters do not speak in chapel, much less demonstrate in front of it. In which we all march in ROTC in full and spotless uniform. In which we go into law school but not into the Peace Corps. In which we make an impact on the larger culture by, say, serving as a coach in the NBA.

My guess now is that what we seldom reckon on is the mind of Christ, which may not want any leaders for tomorrow at all—at least not in the sense that we usually think of them. What I liked so much about that moment in which President Armerding nodded at me was the sense of release. "Go," he said. "Do what the mind of Christ suggests. Whatever the mind of Christ suggests to you, do that." That may not be what he intended, but that's what I will keep on taking. I figure it is up to Jesus to transform our culturally bound gestures, and I'd like to think he transformed that one. On the spot. That the eyes of Hudson Armerding were the eyes of Jesus, looking into the mind of Jesus.

So this is the moment I most want to hold on to—this moment of leaving, this moment of blessing. And even now, if The Boys come knocking on my door—say, at seven o'clock some evening—I hope that I will welcome them home.

The Kahiltna Open:
Scenes from a Climb

Our Room

I CAN STILL SEE THE ROOM. It was dingy, old. A gaudy turquoise carpet held a neatly shaped iron burn at our feet as we opened the door. Barry was my roommate, and his uncle had lived here a generation before. His uncle said the iron burn was new since his time, when Billy Graham had lived down the hall and used to lie on his bed for hours, staring at the naked light bulb.

It was a room for two. Every other slot off the hall contained one lonely male. I knew how lonely—I'd lived in one of those slots at the start of the quarter. My roommate-to-be had been killed on a Texas highway during summer vacation, which made the dirty walls press in on me. Barry had lived next door then with a swimmer he did not much like, I think because the guy got up before dawn to swim and flipped the lights off after sunset. Barry would rather play his electric guitar than tiptoe around Speedo swimsuits hung up in the dark, so he had approached me to switch places with aqua-man.

This worked out to everyone's satisfaction, and I didn't get on Barry's nerves except to tape up mountain photos cut out of *National Geographic* and old bank calendars on all four walls. Then as I held my chemistry book open before me, my eyes would drift to these alpine scenes, and I would sigh. Faraway sighs. Barry was from New Jersey, therefore without pity, and would flatly pronounce, "Read the book." Easy for him to say. How would he know how dull it was in Illinois if he'd never wandered through snowy Cascade peaks or climbed granite Sierra walls? "What do you mean?" Barry would say. "New Jersey has some pretty nice spots."

The nearest alpine props to our room were some bluffs at Devil's Lake, Wisconsin. They reminded me of New Jersey quite a bit—Coney Island Beach tilted ninety degrees. People swarmed these rocks, each one yelling to someone he had never met about a good hold just two feet above her left hand. I would return to our room on Sunday nights with my thoughts in a tangled coil of rope. "Rock and roll," Barry would say. That's the first thing he would say.

Our room had a smell all its own. Many smells, really, which mingled together in a subdued excitement. My running shorts hung over the heating pipes and breathed an aura of honest sweat. Barry's record albums lent the miracle aroma of rayon. Randy Newman smelled the best, probably. Our bunk bed emanated sleep-grimed odors of sheets we forgot to change every Thursday. The textbooks published their smells too—you could put your nose right in the crease between the covers and breathe deep of printed knowledge, available to all the senses. Augustine, Aquinas, Luther—all rich and mellow. But my chemistry text smelled clinically abrupt. I could not have tolerated those pages without the pungent autumn haze sneaking in through the window. The haze spoke of football practices, all but finished save the wind sprints, and of smiling bald professors stalking home through falling leaves. The tingling haze sneaked in past the peeling window-ledge and bounced off the cool gray walls and caught us on the rebounds, delightfully mixed with the full adventure of all parts of our room.

The telephone, however, had no smell. It squatted on the wall by the door in most sterile fashion. The autumn haze had nothing to do with it. We used it a lot—fantastic messages from lands apart would slip through the instrument—but it wasn't part of our room. It was more like a foreign embassy, available yet aloof, teeming with diplomats who whispered strange news and hidden offers.

One night the telephone made an offer from California, without whispers. "How would you like to climb Mt. McKinley?" it said.

"Climb what?" I answered.

"Mt. McKinley? The highest peak on the continent?"

"I'd like to," I said.

I called Mary Austen once and sent a little diplomat scurrying through my foreign embassy in her room to request the honor of her presence at dinner. She politely assured him that she would attend. The dinner was to be in our room. Mary Austen thought it would be in a restaurant. That was our big surprise. Barry and I tried to scrub out the iron burn in the rug and threw my shorts behind the bed. In the center of the room we made a card table with a white tablecloth appear, and in the center of the tablecloth we placed a knifeblade piton inside a little glass case. Randy Newman jumped onto the stereo and Mary Austen swept into the room.

We were faced off on either side of the piton while Barry catered macaroni and cheese with tuxedoed grace. She never asked about the piton, and I was sure she didn't know what it was. Eschewing the rudeness of pointing out her ignorance, I took up a weightier subject.

"You know," I said, "I've been thinking this week that the fall of humankind may in fact have had no intrinsic effect upon nature, and that creation suffered only from our postlapsarian stewardship. Nature could not have been cursed with death, for death is no doubt a created part of nature; and so nature is only fallen insofar as humankind abuses it." It was magnificent, the way it came out. Mary Austen, who I knew was a philosophy major, would be hard pressed for a response.

She responded immediately. "That," she said, "is the stupidest thing I've ever heard. Furthermore, I can take any side of an argument that I please. And win." She glared at me, a twenty-second nonstop glare.

"Hmm," I said. "Maybe you're right. So, how's the mac and cheese? It's my favorite—that's why we're having it."

"Quite dry," she answered, and nudged it to the side of her plate.

She had an uncanny thirst for power, this young woman. We let Randy Newman do the talking for a while. "Let's drop the big one now," he said.

Then I spoke again. "How do you like our room?"

She looked around, then sniffed and wrinkled her nose. "It's a dingy old room," she pronounced.

Form M-87-b

To the examining physician:

The bearer plans to participate in expeditionary mountaineering in Mount McKinley National Park, Alaska. The National Park Service, in the interest of personal safety, wishes to be assured that he is in physical and mental condition to endure the extreme stresses associated with arctic mountaineering.

The climber will probably be carrying heavy loads (often 60-90 lbs.) at altitudes between 10,000′ and 20,000′. Conditions vary from intense snow glare with temperatures as high as 90° F to storms with winds of over 100 MPH and temperatures below −40° F. Expeditions usually last from two to six weeks. Prolonged confinement within cramped tents or snow caves due to bad weather often occurs. Rescue may be exceedingly slow and uncertain in case of serious injury or illness.

Headache, muscle cramps, cough, Cheyne-Stokes breathing, anorexia, digestive disturbances, poor sleep, nervous tension, and intense fatigue are common complaints on the higher climbs in McKinley Park. Serious cold injury (particularly to the feet), snow blindness, acute pulmonary edema of altitude, and direct injuries due to falls, fires in tents, etc., can occur.

In the light of the above, do you feel that the bearer can effectively participate in such an expedition?

The Kahiltna Open

I rolled up a hundred peanut butter balls for our trip. They were about the size of golf balls. When frozen on the Kahiltna Glacier they felt like golf balls, which gave us the sportsman's incentive.

After dinner one night, as the sun was poised for its deep-freeze dive behind Mt. Foraker to the west, we dug a cup-size hole in the ice and marked it with a bamboo wand. Then we assembled a wonderful assortment of clubs: snowshovels as drivers, snowshoes as irons, and a variety of ice axes as putters. One sled, pulled by an able caddy, held the clubs in readiness. It seemed like an easy course, although a bad hook could send the ball into a nearby crevasse.

Eager to try my skill, I stepped up to the tee. "I recommend this Sherpa Lightfoot, Sahib," said my caddy. "Sir Edmund Hillary once scored a hole in one on the eighteenth using this model."

That's good enough for me, I thought, taking the club from my barefoot assistant. I lined up on the ball and shifted my weight as my college P.E. instructor had taught me. "Everyone should learn to play golf," he'd said. "You never know when you'll be asked to play a few rounds with the boss."

I pulled back and swung hard. The ball soared sharply right in a high arc, catching the last rays of the Arctic sun, a flaming comet bound for destiny. At last it plummeted to the glacier, bounced once, and rolled neatly into the crevasse.

"See," I told my caddy. "I was aiming for that, you know."

"Sahib knows best," he said.

An Igloo

Igloos came in handy. We once encountered a three-day blizzard (although you don't know it's a three-day blizzard until it's over and you don't have to encounter it anymore) and pitched our tents in the middle of the vast Kahiltna. Tents are easier to set up than igloos—that's why we set up our tents. Wind blew, snow fell. We cut out salt-lick-size blocks and stacked them wall high to the windward. This would keep snow from drifting over the tents in the night.

That evening the wind and snow blew dirty gray, with grim knuckle-down energy. We sat in our tents burping half-cooked Japanese noodles. All at once the tent walls caved in upon us, and through the little ripstop nylon squares we felt salt-lick-size blocks. And we said, "Hello, wall." We said this because one of us worked at a ski factory with a fellow who faced the wall every day and said, "Hello, wall. Hello, hello wall," in a quite friendly manner. So actually we were quoting.

The wall had broken two poles. We splinted them with bamboo and, rather than rebuild the wall, decided to get up every two hours and dig out the tents. So, every two hours, someone braved the storm and shoveled off the drifted snow. Sometime after midnight, though, everyone fell asleep. How could we have fallen asleep? The tent walls crack-snapped vehemently, like American flags on March afternoons.

I woke up before dawn in a bear hug. If I moved, the tent poles would snap. My tentmate was under the same pressure. We called to the next tent and heard someone throw up. *Expeditions,* I thought. *What are expeditions for?* A shovel squeaked to the rescue, bravely digging a hole through one tent wall. Before the snow was cleared away, another pole crumpled.

I began to think of the sunny south steps of the student union, a chocolate-mint cone in hand, bare feet baking into the warm concrete, ivy-covered dolomite walls rising above green lawns, Frisbees wafting about, professors nodding hello. But it was not time to think; it was time to build an igloo.

We took most of the day to cut rotten blocks from the storm-soft snow and paste them into an in-leaning spiral. There was no air left in the air; it was all displaced by flying snow. As Robert Service famously put it, "When our eyes we'd close our lashes froze / Till sometimes we couldn't see." We stumbled from quarry to igloo, snow blocks crumbling in our hands, fingers numb, feet frozen. Our mason stood within the spiral; we'd hand him our blocks, he'd pack them in place. The mason's skill would be tested when the walls began arching toward each other; that is, when walls became ceiling. He would have to guide them delicately to the final capstone before they collapsed. A partially built igloo would not count.

Our walls closed inward, yearning to meet. Completion looked imminent, yet impossible. By abrogation of the laws of gravity we reached the point where only a head-size hole remained. The wind tore at the hole wildly, shredding away chunks and slivers of snow. We passed the final block through the ground entrance and watched as two mittens popped it out the top, righted it, then settled it down slowly, slowly, like a trap door softly closing.

It stayed.

We quickly burrowed through the entrance, fat little snowmen all, to congratulate our mason. Inside our crystal palace we found heavenly silence; the storm had lost its tonsils. We warmed our hearth with a flaming stove, brewed the good broth, and blessed the hollow ringing in our ears.

Kahiltna Katie

While we wandered up the Kahiltna Glacier on Mt. McKinley, a Japanese expedition was attempting Mt. Foraker. We knew because we heard them on our radio. The word *follicle* kept coming up in their transmissions. This identified their peak, of course, but the metaphor was badly chosen.

Hearing our counterparts through the static bolstered our belief in Kahiltna Katie. At times we were sure we heard her sweet stilted voice coming faintly over the air: "Mountaineer boy—hey there, mountaineer boy. Come bottom of crevasse, have rice soup! Make you safe, make you happy, mountaineer boy." We took pride in steeling ourselves against her beckoning. Yet her invitation came again and again, warming our radio. It was that last "mountaineer boy" that always got to us.

I once came close to meeting Kahiltna Katie on a later climb in the Sierra Nevada of California. While crossing the bergschrund below North Palisade, I quite neatly popped through the snowbridge and found myself in a dazzling cavern, a blue hole of sky some fifty feet over my head. On the snowy floor beside me, a beautiful Asian girl dressed in white sealskin knelt beside a purring stove. The pot smelled rich and steamy.

"You must be Kahiltna Katie," I said, pinching myself.

"Solly," replied the girl. "Katie retire last year. Now live in mobile home in Palm Springs."

"I'm very sorry to hear that," I said.

She looked at me with a Mona Lisa smile and pressed my mitten affectionately. "But Katie ask me to give golf ball back," she whispered.

In my palm was a well-fondled ball of peanut butter, half-thawed. "Thank you," I breathed. "Thank you so much."

"Make you happy, mountaineer boy," she said.

Or Something

One morning, at around fourteen thousand feet, I awoke early and threw up. The vomit froze quickly on my bag and agreeably scraped off. It was bright orange. At least I think it was bright orange—you're never sure what color anything really is inside a yellow tent.

I was then at my leisure to reflect until the others got up, and I threw my full mental energies into solving the problem, *Why climb?* I recalled one professor's slogan about the end of a liberal arts education: "To join the human race and become more fully human." I decided to apply it to mountaineering. It sounded good. There was a fulfilling ring to it. On my way out of camp that morning I popped the question on the one female member of our expedition. She was a nurse.

"Why climb mountains?" I asked.

"I've never thought about it," she said. "Why should you worry about it?"

I carried a load of food up the snowslope above camp that morning. It took three dull hours. There was another person plodding at the other end of the rope. I forget who. It doesn't much matter—a hundred feet of rope isn't all that telepathic. Switchbacking uphill, I saw the tracks ahead, and that's all I saw. The other guy jerked me as I turned corners. I suspected that he had it in for me, that I had become the object of some long-nurtured malice. Pretty soon I was hating him right back, although sometimes I lapsed into a good mood and was merely irritated.

We reached a crevasse, in time, and crossed on a snowbridge—new scenery here to divert rankled thoughts. It looked black down deep, with a deathlike hollowness inside. I peered into the underworld, at once forbidden and forbidding. Then the rope pulled taut, and I was hauled away.

It was not much farther up hard steep snow to a cave we'd dug at the base of our fixed lines. We dumped our packloads in the cave and gazed at the thin line of rope darting up the ice face to the horizon.

Then we turned around. The view was enough to make me feel fully human, insignificantly human. Far below, in the middle of a white void in the cirque of the Kahiltna Glacier, was the dark speck of our camp, resting like a spider on a plastered ceiling. Beyond crowded row after row of snow-mantled giants. Like most of the people who climb on McKinley, I could name only Hunter and Foraker. But then, none of these peaks knew my name either. They probably didn't even know their own names. If they did, they were names unknown to anyone else. But a noble sight, however anonymous we were.

Inspired, I decided to use our two-way radio to call Anchorage, where I could be patched into a telephone and reach Barry in Illinois. Barry answered.

"Hi," I said. "I'm at fifteen thousand feet. You should see the view up here."

Barry didn't even favor me with a stunned silence. "You mean you're not at a telephone booth?" he asked.

Pretty soon he put his new fiancée, Mary Austen, on the phone. She was properly awed and didn't say much. Out of character for her, though. "What's the matter?" I said. "Are you just too amazed to be talking with me?"

The reply came quick and hard. "What are you," she snapped— "an egotist or something?" That was all. More silence. She may have meant it.

That night I got to reciting her question. It echoed around in my altitude-aching head as I tried to sleep, nestled in my sleeping bag with a bulky pair of water bottles, both inner and outer leather boots, damp wool mittens, and six or seven wet socks in an effort to make them warm and dry—or at least to keep them from freezing solid.

"What are you . . . ?"

Garden Stakes

As the expedition proceeded, I studiously plunged green bamboo garden stakes into the snow every 150 feet to mark our path. In a blizzard, you could barely see from one to the next. A grand procession of garden stakes would follow us to the top. Along sown furrows of steps, seed holes would soon sprout. If we didn't return quickly, the way might become wildly overgrown.

Each wand, as they were called, was decorously capped with a little orange flag. I had tied these flags on, one at a time, in the basement at home. My high-school girlfriend had come to help and asked about the girls at college.

"How are the girls at college?" she asked.

I quickly attached one flag to three wands stuck together. Which was crazy—I had nothing to hide. From the summit, perhaps, I would see all the girls from college lined up behind me, carrying little orange flags.

Dr. Livingstone, I Presume

One morning, high on the mountain, I heard British voices outside the tent and feet squeaking on the snow. In the slow stupor of altitude, I took awhile to decide if it was worth getting up to see who was who. When I did crawl out, I saw two figures crouched by a stove. They wore bright blue jumpsuits tucked into sleek orange overboots. Their calves looked enormous.

"Good morning," said I, tentatively.

"Good morning," returned the shorter one. He had long, scraggly hair, which I took to be silver. Then I saw it was brown, flecked with ice. "Have some tea?" he suggested.

"No, thanks," I said and cringed, recalling the time I'd eaten Sunday dinner at a British professor's house and refused the same offer four times. The professor had risen out of his chair, wrinkled his forehead, and demanded, "Will you get civilized and drink some tea with us?" But this fellow with the icy hair evidently wasn't civilized; he just liked tea. He didn't care if I did or not.

"Where are you from?" I asked.

"He's from Edinburgh, I'm from Nottingham."

"Nottingham," I repeated. "As in, *The Sheriff of?*" I got a glacier-goggled stare; a change in subject seemed in order. "And your names?"

"Haston and Scott." He pronounced them crisply, precisely, as if they were a partnership. I realized I had heard these names before, but I couldn't place them. He didn't ask my name.

"And what do you do for a living?"

"Climb," said Scott. "We're professionals, you know. We just did the South Face—six bivouacs, with a variation of our own." He added this last detail with emphasis. They both looked exasperated.

"Amazing," I said. "You must be tired."

Scott seemed bemused and sipped his tea in silence for a while. He nodded toward the summit and murmured, "It's Mordor up there." Then in a scrappy voice, he said, "First brew we've had in a long while. We've run out of fuel messing around with this bloody stove. Just a bag of prunes left. The altitude's got us ringy dingy. We're pretty bloody fucked up, mate."

"Me too," I nodded. We seemed to have something in common.

Mr. Haston had nothing to say. He put in a distant clean-shaven nod now and then, as befits a strong, silent type. On his head sat a gray balaclava that was not stylishly folded—his hair stuck out through the hole on top.

They finished tea, and Scott fumbled with his climbing harness, dropping it three times as he reached between his legs for the elusive crotch strap. Then they staggered unroped toward the West Buttress, Haston in the lead. One of his feet was markedly pigeon-toed.

Even So

Late of an Illinois winter evening, I walked across a creaking parlor and mounted a crimson Victorian chair next to the piano. I reached to a bookshelf above the piano, pulled down *The Tourist's Guide to Mount McKinley,* and turned to a black-and-white aerial photo of the summit. Standing on the chair, I drew a tiny black *X* on the picture at the highest point I had reached, on a little snowy plain near the top. Then I put the book back, got down from the chair, and turned out the lights. From underneath the front door, a bitterly cold wind sifted around my ankles in the dark.

All the Way Down

THOUGH I WAS A LITTLE AFRAID, I asked to go first. By the way that my brother shrugged his shoulders and said "Okay," I could tell he wanted to lead it himself. Ordinarily we would have talked, but our ledge was cold, the mountain high, the day short.

Below us I saw the rest of our party laboring out of the boulderfield. Dave and I were two of ten climbers who had banded together to attempt Alaska's Mt. McKinley in late April. But this was Longs Peak in Colorado, in December—a shakedown climb. After battling snow and high winds for three days we had pitched a camp at the base of the rocky north face, and morning had dawned clear, calm, and below zero. Dave and I had set out early to fix ropes on the steepest part of the route above. It was not steep by summer standards, but in winter shade, at nearly fourteen thousand feet, just tying the end of the rope to my harness was a painful challenge.

Dave anchored himself, belayed the line around his waist, and told me to "git." He would hold me if I fell, but I might fall a long way. That is the risk the leader takes. I clambered up a crack in big double boots, pawing the rock through black silk gloves, and soon made a disheartening discovery. What looked like a film of frost on the face was actually ice—*verglas*—that could not be broken or brushed away. It was climb the ice or not at all.

So I teetered upward, hooking each hold with fingers and soles and pressing them absolutely rigid for fear of the abyss. I moved very slowly, with the wildest kind of faith, clipping the rope from time to time through an old piton or a wedge set in an ice-choked crack to limit the length of a possible plunge. When after a hundred feet or more I reached at last an eye-bolt on a flat ledge, I wrapped my arms about it in gratitude.

Dave led an easier pitch, and by late afternoon we were all grouped on the level summit, looking out on the purple snows of the infinite Rockies. That night we howled and sang in our tents, and I felt myself a bit of a hero. Dave later wrote to a friend on a post card, "We just climbed Longs. Paul led the gnarly stuff." As we headed home for Christmas, I knew what my gift to the group had been.

But this was all prelude to Denali, the great one, four months later. Again we battled wind and snow—this time for three weeks—to establish a high camp under the summit. We left, four of us, well before dawn, on two ropes—I with a quiet, sturdy man, Don Wheeler; Dave with an experienced ranger from Mt. Rainier, John Thompson. John was fairly new to us, but we had led wilderness trips with Don the summer before and had come to value his competence. The others were either nursing illness in camps below or resting for a later attempt.

I have wanted few things more badly in life than to get to the top of McKinley that day. We had a mere three thousand feet to go, basically a long steep walk over snow and ice with sharp-spiked crampons strapped to the soles of our monstrous boots. From the summit I was secretly planning to use our two-way radio to phone my roommate in Illinois. As we headed up the first slope, my steel crampons burning the cold into my feet, I warmed myself with thoughts of what I would say to him.

We spent much of the morning angling up a moderately steep pass between the north and south summits. Near the top of it, my crampons twisted away from my boots in an inconveniently steep spot, and I skittered on to where Don could help me strap them back on, a task that was brutal on mittenless fingers. I might have done it myself, I suppose, but Don did. He was like that. By the time we caught up with Dave and John at the top of the pass, they were eager to push ahead.

We did, and here, just above eighteen thousand feet, I began to enter another world. Walking at a distance from one's companions at the end of a rope is lonely enough. But now I felt removed as in sleep, climbing very slowly, as when one tries to run in a dream, and hearing the voices of the others ahead in a strange, delayed sort of way. So this is altitude, I thought. On the upper reaches of Mt. McKinley, less than half the oxygen at sea level is available to human lungs. Even so, most parties trust to acclimatization, and we were no different. In spite of my new strange lassitude, I knew I would make it.

I did not. After throwing my crampons a few more times and watching in a daze as Don restrapped them, I followed the others over a rise and onto a snowy plain. Just a quarter-mile away the summit rose in a final, simple eight hundred feet—the highest point in North America. For some reason, the way was not clear to the others. I thought I saw it, and took the lead, but not for long. Suddenly I was stumbling in circles, falling down. The altitude had won.

The others caught up. "I have to go down," I said, and wept. We had planned the expedition for a year and a half. I had taken the quarter off from college, used up my savings to buy the gear. It had come to this.

A powwow resulted, and Don volunteered to accompany me. John and Dave climbed on—and I did not blame them—planning to rejoin us shortly on the descent. They did not return for three days, and when they did they were horribly frostbitten. And that is a whole other story.

I think now of my staggering down on Don's heels, sprawling in the snow again and again, and feeling his arms lift me up yet one more time. By then I was hallucinating, no longer on Mt. McKinley but stumbling along a logging road in the Cascades. When dark came, Don chipped a trench in the ice with his ax and bundled me into it next to him. By dawn our fingertips were black. He spoke to me patiently, put on my crampons, and led me down once again. Where the going was steep he sent me ahead on a tight rope, and more than once I pulled him pell-mell after me toward deep crevasses. By midmorning we reached our high camp, and as I lay in the tent it came to me that someone—one person in particular—had saved my life.

This all happened long ago, and neither then nor now would Don Wheeler think of himself as particularly heroic. I think of him whenever I read Wordsworth's lines on "that best portion of a good man's life; / His little, nameless, unremembered acts / Of kindness and of love." For Don, strapping on crampons was just another way of washing feet. For many years not a month went by without my dreaming I had made it to the summit. But I have that dream less frequently now, and it is just as well. It is less important that I led the way for everyone up Longs Peak than that someone led the way for me down Mt. McKinley.

One Fine Morning

SONYA THE HORSE had a long black lock that hung down her forehead over one eye or the other. "Your hair's getting long," I told her that morning. "Aren't you afraid of missing an easy layup in the big game?"

This was absurd. In Yosemite, horses don't play basketball. So Dave smiled through his red beard as he gathered up the saddle. "Answer him, Sonya," he said. I liked to see my brother smile. More often he looked worried.

He had his reasons. Month after month, summer after summer, he kept track of as many as five groups at a time in the High Sierra of California, each group wending a separate course through the backcountry (and I usually helping with one of them). Dave, you see, ran a wilderness program. Each group of trekkers was led by experienced mountaineers, but it was up to Dave to plan the maze of routes, and it was up to Sonya and Dave to find and resupply each group about a week into their trip. Above all it was up to Dave (and maybe Sonya) to worry.

Let me count the ways. For starters, people could drown in streams, freeze in snowstorms, fall down glaciers, plunge off cliffsides. Even our staff could accomplish such things. Just the summer before, an incautious leader had stepped on a loose rock and surfed two hundred feet over a precipice. He was nursed through the night, a bloody heap on a cold ledge, while two boys ran fourteen miles out for a helicopter. Dave and Sonya worried about things like that.

Just now it was the weather. It was a fine canyon morning—autumn blue, autumn silent. But the past three days had brought thunderous rain, then hail, then snow. Flakes had whirled and clung to the peaks and high valleys, stinging the granite, filling the meadows, bowing tarps to the ground on gray leaden mornings. One girl got so dangerously cold that someone was stuffed in a sleeping bag with her. You joked about that treatment—until the time came.

To that group Dave had brought a winter tent. Then he rode down from the snow onto trails edged by amber meadows, down from the snow into granite canyons with pillow-smooth walls. He stayed for me in a lodgepole stand, stopping by the woods on a starry evening. We talked that night by the quiet stream where the moon reflected off still pools and polished stone banks. Dave said the day had reminded him of another snowy ride with Sonya, two Septembers before. Both times, as they plodded through the hush, the snowflakes settling on Sonya's mane, they had surprised a doe and her fawn in a thicket. Both times the doe had fled to distract them, and both times the fawn stood glassy-eyed on quivering legs while Sonya braced each hoof.

Now, in the morning, Sonya stood unconcerned before me while Dave tightened the girth strap under her belly. I patted her nose in strained familiarity—"There Sonya, there Sonya"—but she knew and I knew we were just bare acquaintances. The few times I had ridden her she had sensed great lack of authority in the saddle. She nudged up and down my chest now, then caught her nose solidly in my crotch.

"What's that mean?" I asked.

Dave laughed. "You can fantasize about a relationship if you want," he said, "but it means her nose itches."

Sonya pawed and snorted, and I reached one hand up to the decayed sweet warmth of her nostrils. Dave was cackling through his nose now—that most wicked of laughs—while fiddling some more with the buckle under her belly. He was having a hard time with the buckle—he had come back from Denali four years before without fingers or feet.

At the time, it was still called Mt. McKinley. We were more than four years younger then, and all the world was worth a college try. I remember collapsing fatigued on that snowfield, watching Dave and one other climb on toward the top, the snowy top in the dark blue haze, so close I could touch it with the tip of my frozen mitten. Surely they would make it, I thought. But a few steps below the summit, Dave's partner collapsed. Minutes later Dave's bivouac gear blew away. It was thirty below zero. They survived the night in a shallow ice trench, stumbled downward, bivouacked again, and at last found rescue. The doctors said they should have died up there.

That was spring, and the summer would have been Dave's fifth to lead groups in the Sierra. Instead he lay on a bed and watched his extremities rot in a black stench. In midsummer they chopped away the mummified remains: each finger, each thumb, over half of each foot. "Look, Ma," he grimly said. "No hands."

Once out of the hospital it was wheelchairs, crutches, and then—most profoundly—Sonya. It wasn't that he couldn't stump around a bit on his own—they gave him special shoes for that. And he grew wonderfully adept with his paws, getting to where he could tie a bowline tolerably well. But he couldn't walk far and he couldn't walk fast. You can't manage in the mountains any other way. A friend sold Sonya to Dave for a song, and so began a three-years' ride through northern Yosemite—saddlebags jammed with crampons for one group, five days' tuna and gorp for another, and a sack of rusty cans he'd found at some lake. Hidden at the bottom of one saddlebag might be a small watermelon. Sometimes you would see Sonya patiently hitched to a windblasted juniper while Dave labored the last half-mile up talus to a summit. In his own words, Sonya was a most faithful woman.

"Want help with that buckle?" I asked, knowing his answer. He grunted and slid the metal tongue through the leather himself. I helped clip on the saddlebags with his rusty carabiners, then stuffed a climbing rope down beneath a broken zipper—snug where it wouldn't fall out. By the look in Dave's eyes, I knew he thought I might need the rope for some oddball rescue attempt in the days ahead. He would rather I kept it.

"Don't worry," I told him.

Then he was mounted, and the September sun gleamed off silky granite and Sonya's cream-brown chest. "Goodbye," I said. Dave nodded and clip-clopped Sonya around through the lodgepoles. He bobbed naturally erect, and Sonya slid easily by the trees, almost like a prancing cat.

If the weather held, they would make it to the Hunewill Ranch in a long day's ride, and Dave would let Sonya into the starlit pasture. Perhaps Sawtooth Ridge would still be glowing above them after the sunset. Dave might drop in at the Cedar Tavern in Bridgeport and play shuffleboard with the bartender, sailing the disks quietly through the sawdust. They make a barely audible click when they collide, and then one hangs on the edge of the table for a frozen moment before dropping into the gutter with a silent thud.

Two days passed, and strong winds wailed in the canyons, skidding the peaks through the clouds. Tarps billowed crazily in our hands. We gusted through talus like dominoes, and on the passes we reeled at the crack of invisible whips. Miles beyond our ken, one girl did what we could have done: she fell and smashed her ankle on a boulder. She was carried by her group to a trail by nightfall. Early in the morning, her leader hiked out for some horsepower. Dave was nowhere around, so the leader went alone to the Hunewill place for Sonya.

Sonya was hard to get. There at the ranch, she danced skittishly about the pasture with a crazy moon-eyed horse, determined to enjoy the morning, disdaining to come and be saddled. A half-hour of chasing her didn't work. The Hunewill hands joined in at last, riding and circling the horses until the pair was forced into a wooden corral. Still no good—the moon-eyed horse smashed through the wooden gate, bursting it to kindling, and Sonya followed after.

But Sonya did not escape. In midstride she stopped in surprise and stood dumbly in the ruined gate. A giant wooden splinter wagged strangely from her neck, stuck in her jugular vein. She was spurting her life away. It took twenty minutes.

I was standing with Dave in the trailhead dust when they told him the news. His face knotted up like the whorls on a whitebark snag above timberline. We heard the details—her glazed eyes, her quivering legs, the hand heel-deep in her neck's blood. We heard how she collapsed to the ground, how she jumped up again to try to escape whatever it was, how she collapsed the last time, spraying the grass crimson. We heard this, but that's not what we saw, because so much of death is our last glimpse of life. Perhaps Dave saw a trembling fawn, and steaming breath, and snow melting on her mane. I saw her nudging and snorting, hair in her eyes, one man on her back. Sonya's blood spurted into that fine canyon morning, and saddling her up became larger than loss.

THE VALLEY

Why are you cast down, O my soul,
and why are you disquieted within me?

—Psalm 42:5

Inspirational Romance

SOME YEARS AGO my sister-in-law sent me a set of guidelines for how to write an "Inspirational Romance." She had received them from an evangelical publisher—which one, I'm still not sure. I have to admit I was curious about what the guidelines would suggest. I quote them here, nearly in their entirety:

> The *Wherefore-Art-Thou Series* offers to the discriminating reader books characterized by an intriguing story line, with no offensive speech, behavior, or philosophy. All elements of the books in this line will reflect an evangelical world view with an emphasis on romantic love from the Christian perspective.

> CHARACTERS: The *heroine* should be a young woman between the ages of 24 and 35. She may be beautiful, merely attractive, or even plain—with true beauty emerging as a result of inner resources and/or love that literally transforms her outward

appearance. She may be wholesomely seductive, with an inherent but unpracticed sensuality. In keeping with contemporary lifestyles, she would probably be a working girl; however, career advancement is not necessarily a primary goal. The heroine may or may not be a Christian at the outset. If not, she must be profoundly and positively affected by the Christian values of some other character, probably the hero.

The *hero* should be strong and assertive, a combination of the "tough and tender" personality admired by many women. Professionally, he could be anything from a businessman to a wealthy playboy who later "reforms," from a clergyman to a blue-collar worker. To allow for glamorous and exotic settings, however, at least one of the protagonists should be affluent, with wealth derived from inheritance or earning power.

Secondary characters: While the main action of the plot must revolve around the two leading characters, minor characters are important in providing complication: i.e., the "other woman or man" who vies for the affections of the hero or heroine; a clinging parent; dependent siblings, etc. These secondary characters can be quite vividly portrayed and are necessary to the development of the plot, but care should be taken not to introduce more than three or four significant secondary characters.

SETTING: The locale might be any city, town or rural community in North America, but an international setting is acceptable as long as the main characters are American. Surroundings, whatever the location, should be conducive to romance and intimacy—candlelight, firelight, music, fine foods, cruise ships, etc.

PLOT: A simple love story, expertly told, can be deeply moving and inspirational. A series of complicating factors, both physical (external) and spiritual (internal), must ensue before a resolution is reached, culminating in a *happy ending.*

In addition to the developing love relationship between the protagonists (one of whom must possess strong faith), there should be an underlying spiritual theme which evolves naturally from the storyline. As the relationship deepens, the weaker character should be brought to a realization of his/her need for or growth in Christ, and this problem is then resolved along with the denouement of the plot. Since the practice of Christian principles provides the resources for resolving conflict, these principles can be easily integrated into the story. . . .

TREATMENT OF LOVE SCENES: In this genre, there will be inevitable moments of sexual tension between the lead characters. Description of kissing and embracing are permitted within the bounds of good taste. The ability of the hero and/or heroine to observe certain limits—i.e., prevent sexual feelings from overpowering them—is an essential distinctive of the Christian romance. The difference between lust and love should be noted.

After being enlightened by such a helpful set of directions, I couldn't resist writing my own Inspirational Romance. Since the guidelines allow for a setting in any rural community in North America, I selected the desert town of Bridgeport, California. For my heroine I chose an old friend named Georgia. Georgia worked with a number of us, including a fellow named Sven, in a small mountaineering program called Sierra Treks. She had a boyfriend named Ted who was studying to be a psychologist; he had an annoying habit of showing up at our basecamp in

Bridgeport between our trips into Yosemite. So I chose Ted for my romance hero.

[The curtain opens with our heroine and hero waiting in the Bridgeport City Park for their trekkers to arrive for the start of a trip. The two sit opposite one another at a picnic table, a bit pensive. A mournful wind blows through the sagebrush behind them.]

GEORGIA: We've got to stop meeting like this, Ted. What do you mean by gagging and tying Sven and locking him in the bathroom at the Trails Restaurant? We're sure to be found out. Even with his red bandanna on you'll never pass for him.

TED: Fear not, my princess. The Boss will never know the difference. By this clever scheme we shall enjoy the next twelve days in the backcountry in perfect bliss, my sweetest.

GEORGIA [astonished]: Why, you're so strong and assertive, so—so tough and tender. Already you have solved one physical (external) complicating factor in our romance. [She pauses.] Are you sure The Boss won't see you?

TED: I'm sure. He's too busy editing his new magazine, *Good Horsekeeping.*

GEORGIA [flying into his arms and embracing in good taste]: Oh, my dearest! You wealthy playboy, you. Ah, let us note the difference between love and lust. But wait a minute. [She draws back.] Just how affluent are you, anyway?

TED: Don't worry, princess. I have glamorous wealth derived from both inheritance and earning power. Whatever you like—firelight, candlelight, music, fine foods, cruise ships—I am well able to provide. Name any exotic setting you desire that is conducive to romance and intimacy. What is your wish, my sweet?

GEORGIA [reflectively]: You know, with all my heart I wish that someday I could lead the summit block of the Doodad on Sawtooth Ridge. Then I could be a *real* Treks guide.

TED [in horror]: Georgia, you don't mean—gasp!—that career advancement is one of your primary goals! I think you have just introduced an internal complicating factor in our relationship. You, of all people! You, Georgia, so wholesomely seductive, with such an inherent but unpracticed sensuality, wanting to lead the Doodad!

GEORGIA: Sorry, Ted, but in keeping with contemporary lifestyles, I'm a working girl. [She reaches into her pocket.] See? Here's my green card.

TED: Your green card! Georgia, this is not allowable. Don't you realize you absolutely must be an American to take part in our romance? Next you're going to tell me you're a Democrat!

GEORGIA: Hold it, Ted. What's that suspicious-looking book in your pocket?

TED: Tut-tut. Just a little volume of Nietzsche. Some light reading for solo day.

GEORGIA: Nietzsche! I will have no offensive philosophy in our romance! I won't have it! [She turns away and pouts.]

TED: Come come, Georgia, act your age. Hold on—how old are you, anyway?

GEORGIA: I'll be thirty-six tomorrow. What are you going to get me for my birthday?

TED: Ah, that's bad, that's bad. One year over the acceptable limit for heroines—yet another complicating factor. At this rate, how shall we ever reach a resolution, effect a denouement, and culminate in a *happy ending*? What's more, didn't I see you with Bigfoot the other day? How come you've never told me about him, Georgia?

GEORGIA: I don't know. I didn't want to get carried away, I guess. Wait! What's this under the table? [She looks.] Why, if I didn't know better, I'd say it was your mother, Ted, secretly holding your hand the whole time. What could be more disgusting than a clinging parent?

TED: Careful, Georgia. That makes four significant secondary characters we have introduced. I will admit that Sven, The Boss, Bigfoot, and my mother are quite vividly portrayed and that they are necessary to the development of the plot, but care should be taken not to introduce more.

GEORGIA: Look! Someone's coming! I think it is the kindly old widow, Mrs. Bryant, who runs the local motel in this rustic but charming high desert village of Bridgeport, California.

TED: Oh no! That makes five! We're done for! And who is the other woman with her?

GEORGIA: Ted, did you say *the other woman*? It is! I'm so hurt. I never recognized her before her outward appearance was transformed.

TED: Horrors! Here comes Sven too, and The Boss is with him.

GEORGIA: Fly, Ted, fly! I'm afraid it's all over with us. Lie low at the Hunewill Ranch until I return. Who knows, perhaps our love can live again.

TED: I am gone, my sweet—destined to eat nothing but baked beans in your absence. Ah, farting is such sweet sorrow.

[He leaps over the barbed-wire fence and races off through the sagebrush, only slightly encumbered by his clinging parent. As the curtain closes, our heroine wipes away a tear and forces an enigmatic smile.]

Strange, is it not, the things we admit in the writing of our Inspirational Romance? But I must admit just one thing more. On a winter climb in the Clark Range, just back of Yosemite Valley, I met a young woman who dropped a mitten hundreds of feet down the snowy headwall of a mountain.

"I'll just get that for you," I told her.

"You will?" she said.

With a flourish of my ice ax, I plunge-stepped down the steep slope and reached the mitten with relative ease. After climbing back up, I presented it to her nonchalantly. She glowed with appreciation, we continued on to a splendid summit, and that night, perched on a shelf carved high on a sinuous ridge, together we melted pot after pot of sugar-loose snow on a flaming stove while the rest of our group curled up in their tents.

The stars that night—we seemed among them. And the deep, cold silence that spread out over the domes and forests at our feet. What can I say? Just this. Reader, I married her.

Spokane: A Triptych

I Should Have Talked

IN HIS BOOK *Desert Solitaire*, Edward Abbey refers offhandedly to American evangelicalism as a form of mental illness. I am hoping he is wrong. And it seems to me that Abbey himself, in his many barbs directed at his childhood faith, cannot quite turn his eyes away from it. In this, I think, he is like Mark Twain—both of them Christ-haunted in twisted and peculiar ways. If there is a mental illness of faith, there may also be a mental illness of lost faith.

But Abbey's comment invites agreement, even from evangelicals. At the very least, evangelicalism seems to encourage strange forms of delusional, masochistic behavior. This literally came home to me some years ago, during the time my wife and I were still in school, when a sadly afflicted man spent the night with us in Spokane, Washington. Sharon and I picked him up on a grimy winter afternoon at the bus station. He had come from Pullman, eighty miles south. His wife, Jill, an acquaintance of Sharon, had asked if Jerry could stay overnight before flying out to Toronto. I had met Jerry the month before, just before we had moved north to Spokane. He had been witnessing door to door with booklets from the Seventh-day Adventist Church and had knocked on our door as well. One look at his weak eyes and childlike face and I knew he was a little off. Sharon told me she didn't know all the details, but Jill had told her that Jerry was now mentally ill and hadn't held a job for the last two years. They lived on unemployment.

Jerry stepped off the bus carrying a bulging suitcase with broken clasps; it was held together with knotted twine. He spoke softly, ending almost every sentence with *you know*. "I appreciate this, you know." We drove to our apartment, where he sat on the couch and said little. "That's what I do most, you know," he said during dinner. "Just sit on the couch. Don't seem to have the energy." While helping me to wash the dishes, he confided that he planned to enter the ministry. It was hard to know how to reply.

When we finished the dishes, he said, "I'd like to join you in your family worship later this evening, you know."

"Well," I replied, "we were just planning to study tonight, actually."

"We have family worship every night," he said. "We sing some familiar choruses and the kids say their memory verses, you know. Jamie, he can usually say his, but Jay can usually only recognize his verse. Jay's just two, you know. You and Sharon could just pick out some familiar choruses for later on this evening, you know."

As I think about it now, I realize how little it would have cost us to read some Scripture and sing some songs with Jerry that night. I'd like to think that today I would have done so. But on that night, out of pure stubbornness, I suppose, not to mention several poems I had to read for my seminar on the pastoral, I ignored his request. At some level, I felt a kind of creeping revulsion. The idea of family worship felt tainted by his mental illness.

When Jerry saw that Sharon and I were intent on our schoolwork, he left to go witnessing in the neighborhood. I cringed as the door closed behind him. What had we unleashed on our block? Earlier in the evening he had told me about a man on the bus with whom he had shared the gospel. "I offered him the booklet and he took it," he said with a hopeful look.

Over Christmas Jerry had been in the hospital for tests. He had spent several hours lying in a room with a tube all the way down his throat. Next to him had been a man about to go into surgery. A month later Jerry heard fourth hand about a man who had died at the hospital. Jerry was sure it was the man he had lain next to for those few hours.

"I should have talked to him," he said. "I've learned my lesson now—I should have talked to him."

"How could you have talked to him with a tube down your throat?" I asked.

"I should have talked to him," Jerry said.

When Jerry got back from witnessing, he returned a call from his wife. "I love you, honey," he said and then laughed a three-beat, quiet, crazy, embarrassed laugh: "Hee-hee-hee." A minute later he said, "I love you, honey. Hee-hee-hee." He said it exactly the same way.

Then Jerry went out to run for exercise. He wore his winter coat, checked slacks, and leather street shoes. He wouldn't borrow my tennis shoes and sweat pants. Soon enough he came back and took a shower and padded around in his pajamas. Just before going to bed, he settled down for a little while and read a book called

The Christian Father. The next day he would fly to Canada to stay with his parents for a month. I hoped that when I drove him to the airport in the morning we could have some kind of friendly talk. I think I felt ashamed of myself for not warming up to him.

In the morning, however, the streets were thick with fresh snow. Getting Jerry to the airport was suddenly going to be a challenge. As best I could I put on our ancient chains. We drove through fishtailing traffic on the interstate, my arms rigid, and a loose set of links on the left rear tire mercilessly flogged the fender. The whole way there, I didn't say a word.

Just this morning, twenty years later, I happened to have breakfast with a couple who have taken care of five mentally handicapped adults in their home for the last fifteen years. *What manner of love is this?* I thought. Other friends have done this kind of thing as well—even an English professor friend—and my wife has worked off and on in group homes for the retarded. And of course there is the famous example of Henri Nouwen, the Catholic theologian who devoted the last years of his life to serving the mentally disabled.

Perhaps it is true that evangelicalism in its more extreme forms offers a ready means of expression for the unhinged among us. But perhaps it is more true that the mentally ill offer to us the plainest picture of ourselves, our deepest longing for a love we hope both to know and to share. If so, I hope I get another try.

And You Visited Me

When I showed up for my two-o'clock tutorial with Dr. Jordan, I found he was gone. A note on the door said he was ill. So I went across the street to the university library to ask his wife, a librarian, how he was doing. Not well, she said, and gave me the name of a hospital near Spokane, eighty or ninety miles away. I knew he was not a healthy man, but she wasn't very clear about the details of his illness. Would he like a visitor? Since I lived in Spokane, it would not be difficult for me to see him. His wife said a visit might be just the thing. But she didn't look me in the eye.

So three days later, after I had returned home from my weekly stint of tutorials and seminars, I drove out to the named hospital. It rested on the north shore of a quiet lake among ponderosas, spreading lawns, and mossy granite outcroppings. I parked the car and walked past a brown-brick wing behind a row of cedar trees. At the visitor registration desk I gave my name and asked to see Rath Jordan.

The receptionist looked through her papers and said, "I'm sorry, but there is no Rath Jordan here."

I asked her to check again.

"No, sorry. No one by that name."

"There must be some mistake," I said.

"No mistake," she said less pleasantly.

But I didn't leave, and eventually she left her desk and disappeared into another room behind her.

When I had proposed a tutorial in the short story in January, Dr. Jordan had responded to me with a similarly abrupt *no*. He was too busy trying to complete a freshman introduction to literature text for Random House, which, he informed me, two other professors in the department had dropped in his lap because they were too damn lazy to keep up their end of the work. "In two years, neither of them ever wrote a single word." He said *a single word* with slowed, staccato emphasis.

Furthermore, he was too ill to do a study with me. His pancreas and adrenal glands did not function properly, and as a result his body chemistry was precarious. Periodically he would lose all "higher cognitive function." As it was, his mind did not work properly until noon. So there would be no tutorial. That was clear.

Could he recommend other professors, key readings? He went down the list of names carefully: "Too limited in his reading; no real penetration of thought; more of a writer than a critic." No, he couldn't fully recommend anyone. Then he pulled out one book, another, and another, warmed to his most favorite of subjects, waxed eloquent, gained in his face a glow of passion. I excused myself to turn in a paper and then returned. He looked up like a boy who has just decided to play hooky.

"Let's do it," he said.

And so we met for an hour and a half, every Tuesday afternoon. By March we had read Chekhov, Crane, Verga, Fitzgerald. Chekhov was his love.

"'The Lady with the Pet Dog,'" he liked to say, "was Chekhov's way of telling Tolstoy how life really worked. You can't impose a smug moral order the way Tolstoy does in *Anna Karenina*."

"Yes," I liked to reply, "but what if Chekhov has subtracted something that Tolstoy did not impose but merely recognized as inherent?"

After a long wait, the receptionist returned from the back room with surprising evidence of the existence of Rath Jordan. She gave me directions to his ward, where I met him in an old, dirty hallway. He was fully clothed, thin, and pale, and shook my hand warmly. Odd-looking people sauntered about, also dressed in street clothes. They wore strange gazes and expressions. It very belatedly dawned on me what kind of hospital this was. Dr. Jordan ushered me into a dusty lounge, and we sat down on some grimy rubber furniture in playschool blues and greens and yellows. An AM radio blared, and several men played billiards on a battered table.

"Sorry I missed my appointment on Tuesday," he said, "but my body chemistry went completely topsy-turvy. When that happens, I become unavoidably suicidal."

I started inside, but tried not to show it.

"I've just been released from seventy-two hours of intensive observation—along with some pretty hard-core people. I talked to a guy this morning who wired a shotgun under a store manager's throat. He connected the trigger to his own hand with an electrical cord. When the police gunned him down, he automatically set off the shotgun."

I wondered why he was telling me this. Was it to show that he himself was not so deranged as that—or to show that we all were?

"We line up for medication here," he said. "Just like in the *Cuckoo's Nest*. I feel like I'm in that movie sometimes."

I had brought a volume of Fitzgerald, just in case he wanted to talk literature. He did—very badly. We arranged for a small, dingy coffee room to ourselves. It had one, tall, narrow window of many small panes; I wondered if the latticework was an iron grill. We managed a discussion about one Fitzgerald story, "The Diamond as Big as the Ritz," and then he wandered onto the turf of other writers. Clearly, he enjoyed talking. Every once in a while I would interject an observation apropos to the subject he had happened upon. He would stop and say, "Yes, I hadn't thought of that. Very good!" I suppose that this return to the role of caretaker felt reassuring to him. The spell was broken only once, by an attendant with a paper cup of water and a pair of pills. He took them obediently.

Soon afterward our time ended. He put his hand to his head and said, "You'd better leave. I'm getting tired. I can handle being intellectually tired—that's one thing. Or being physically tired—that's almost pleasant. It's being emotionally wiped out that gets me."

He asked if I could come back every other day—he'd have to be here two weeks. "We'd get a lot done that way," he said. Then he apologized for not having reviewed the stories. He wasn't allowed any books.

"I'll let you borrow this one," I offered.

"Okay," he said. "I think I can keep it locked up safe."

Before I left he took me by the arm and said how good it was that I had come. He held my gaze, and his eyes were weak and watery. "If anyone asks about me," he said less certainly, "tell them I'm getting much better and hope to be back soon."

Amo, Amas, Amat

In those student years that we lived in Spokane, Sharon and I eventually moved to a blonde-brick apartment house just west of downtown. Just across the hall from us lived an elderly couple from Plentywood, Montana. Henry Raaen was a Norwegian bachelor farmer until the age of forty-nine, when he married Minnie, a schoolteacher. She had played the organ at the Lutheran church where he had sung in the choir. They celebrated their fiftieth anniversary the summer after we met them. Then Mr. Raaen turned one hundred, and Mrs. Raaen a spry eighty-seven.

One evening they invited us over for dessert, and by request I brought along my textbook for the Latin I was starting to learn. Mrs. Raaen had been a passionate teacher of Latin, and she often complained, or gloated rather, that young people these days were no longer interested in the Latin tongue. When I handed her my text, she found a line in the preface that she read to us with sad glee: "It is notorious that every year increasing numbers of students enter college without Latin."

She turned the pages slowly, looking up to tell us about a former teacher of her acquaintance who could not speak of the death of Julius Caesar without breaking into tears. "Sometimes," said Mrs. Raaen, "I lie awake at night reviewing my conjugations."

Then she got to the first set of verbs in the book. "Oh, yes," she said approvingly. Then, "Henry, do you remember the first conjugation?"

Up to this point, Henry had held a rigid silence. Part blind, part deaf, chock full of arthritis, he nevertheless sat tall and erect in a bright red sweater and tie. The tops of his ears held deep, pale wrinkles. I wondered how his hundred-year-old mind worked.

He answered his wife like a cannon shot: *"Amo-amas-amat-amamus-amatis-amant!"*

Mrs. Raaen paged through the text for another five minutes, fondly absorbed. "Yes," she said, "I recognize most of the words on every page. But it would be too hard to get it all back. Too hard now to get it all back." Her face and voice were sadly resigned.

"May I make a motion," croaked Mr. Raaen, "that we put the Latin aside and proceed with dessert?"

Mrs. Raaen agreed, but then she happened upon the vocabulary index in the back and the keyed exercises that go with every lesson. Dessert did not come for some time.

A few weeks later we invited the Raaens to our apartment to listen to *A Prairie Home Companion* on the radio. We thought they would be the perfect audience. For two hours they sat with us politely in our living room, the volume turned up very high, while Garrison Keillor said droll things about Lutherans and

Norwegian bachelor farmers. Mr. and Mrs. Raaen gave the program their complete and stolid attention. They never laughed. They never smiled. When Garrison Keillor at last said, "Good night, everybody. Good night, now," Henry and Minnie rose to their feet with a kind of puzzled dignity and thanked us for having them. Then they left. *Exuent ambo.*

We later moved just upstairs from them, and from time to time we would hear a crash from below, indicating that Mr. Raaen had fallen off the toilet or out of bed. I would hurry downstairs and recollect Mr. Raaen into something like tranquillity, and life would go on. Periodically an ambulance would come to the door, an occasion that Mrs. Raaen always met with sureness and solemnity. She would follow the stretcher out the door with head held high, arm in arm with the paramedic. This was it, she was thinking. After all these years, the final act, and she would march out like royalty. The fact that she got to repeat this performance several times in no way lessened the effect. She only improved with practice.

A few weeks before Mr. Raaen turned 103, just before Christmas, Sharon gave birth to our first child, a baby boy. Soon after we had brought him home, we took Jonathan down to the Raaens' apartment and into their bedroom, where Mr. Raaen lay cadaverously beneath the covers. With some effort he propped himself up and stretched out a hand of blessing upon the head of our little son. Consider then this giant man, well over six feet in length, with huge, horny, spreading hands. Could Simeon in the temple, when he met with the holy infant, have looked or acted any other way?

Then Mr. Raaen held out a five-dollar bill that he had hidden in the blankets. "From the oldest man in the building to the youngest!" he shouted.

That next year, of course, he died.

Nunc dimittis servum tuum Domine,
Secundum verbum tuum in pace.

Lord, now let your servant depart,
According to your word, in peace.

But Basney Says

In Memoriam Lionel Basney, 1946-1999

WHEN IT SEEMED I MIGHT actually finish my Shakespeare dissertation, I asked my brother Dave, who was recruiting for the Oregon Extension of Trinity College, to keep his eye out for teaching positions. He reported back that someone named Lionel Basney was due to leave the English Department of Houghton College in western New York for a stint at Calvin College in Michigan. I had never heard of Lionel Basney, and all he meant to me in that moment was personal opportunity. Exit Basney. Enter Willis.

When I flew out to Houghton for an interview, I can't say that I learned much more about him. A small man, Lionel kept quietly in the background while I sweated my way through a number of question-and-answer sessions. But I did sense that people were sorry that he was leaving.

I returned to Houghton in July with Sharon and our newborn son. Lionel had yet to leave, and that was when I got to spend some time with him. By then I knew he had grown up in Houghton, that he'd gotten his Ph.D. at the University of Rochester at something like the age of twenty-one, and that he was generally regarded as the most brilliant person on the faculty. (His colleagues told me that he directed Shakespeare plays in his spare time, gave poetry readings from memory, and lectured without notes while sitting calmly cross-legged on a desk. No one could think of a book he hadn't read.) What I knew about myself was that the ink was barely dry on my dissertation at age twenty-nine and that I had never taught a literature course in my life. Hopefully, Lionel could give me a few pointers before he departed.

When I dropped by his house one August evening, the movers were dismantling the piano in their living room. His wife, Ruth, was anxious about this, and Lionel was comforting her. I stood by uncomfortably for a good while. Then, the piano safely stowed on the truck, he took me down the street to where some locals were gathered outside a gas station; the station was going out of business. The little crowd was laconically bidding at auction, and we stood and watched till the last bald tire had been sold. That's all we did that night. I was hoping for a little help on my eighteenth-century syllabus, but no such luck.

Lionel left, classes began, and I plunged into my lectures. I began to gain a little confidence, to realize I had a thing or two to say. But one day, midsentence, talking about Pope or Swift, I was interrupted by a student who didn't even raise her hand. She began her comment, "But Basney says . . ." A week or two later the same thing happened, a different student this time: "But Basney says . . ." I don't remember now what it was that Basney said. I just remember that it made a lot more sense than what I was saying.

I told someone else on the faculty about this student response, and he told Lionel. I think Lionel felt some concern for me—care, even. The next time I saw him, he took me aside and dramatically recited the last lines of "Mac Flecknoe," a mock-epic poem by Dryden. In the poem, the worst poet in the world gives his blessing to his successor, as Elijah does to Elisha. Instead of being taken up into heaven, the older poet ignominiously falls through a trapdoor into the earth:

> Sinking he left his drugget robe behind,
> Born upwards by a subterranean wind.
> The mantle fell to the young prophet's part,
> With double portion of his father's art.

When Lionel recited these lines, I think he wanted to give me permission to be myself. And permission to fail, if that's what it took. Despite the way that some of us put Lionel on a pedestal, I doubt he ever felt like much of a shining success himself. But he gave me a little courage when I sorely needed it. For that I thank him.

Lattice Bridge Road

Houghton, New York

THIS AFTERNOON I RIDE my bike south on Route 19 to Caneadea, past an old farmer sitting at a table heaped with sweet corn for sale. We had some recently: sweet indeed, and almost tender. An elderly neighbor drives by, waves to me in his rearview mirror, pulls into the rutted driveway beside the table. I bet he knows the farmer.

At Caneadea I double back north on the Lattice Bridge Road and cross a steel-grated span over the Genessee River. The water lies dark and still below the grating. If anything, the leaves on the surface are blowing upstream in the breeze. On the east shore, dirt cliffs of fifty feet or so rise above the sumac. As usual, they strike me as a bit pathetic. Yosemite, Yosemite, why hast thou forsaken me?

A quiet afternoon, a gravel road, tall corn, a few cows, barns, farmhouses. Thick hillside of woods on the east now, glimpses of the silent river on the west. At one point I see the white belfry of Fancher Hall, the signature emblem of my current place of employment, hovering in dark green forest across the river. There is no campus, apparently, just the mast of a low-lying ship poking above the waves. It looks tiny, incidental, in the summer ocean of trees and pastures washing about. So easily it could be gone; so recently, perhaps, it was not there.

Two dogs rush out, a small brown mutt and a healthy Dalmatian. I slow, act calm, feel scared. The Dalmatian bites me on the calf—I feel his teeth and pull up my feet as if trying to keep them dry. I am afraid to look.

A pickup passes me, then stops, waits. "Did he break the skin?" asks the man in the cab. His face is weathered, wizened. The bare arm resting on the door is minus a hand.

I look at my leg. "Just toothmarks," I say.

The man gives me his card. He is a timber buyer from Hunt, near Nunda. "If you have trouble, I saw it happen. The guy can't say he had his dog tied up."

A ways further, a bronze tablet on a boulder beside the road. The sort you never stop for when driving. The tablet commemorates the ordeal of one Major Moses Van Campen, "a soldier of the Revolution," who in 1782 was captured by the Senecas and made to run the gauntlet from this spot 30 rods west to an ancient council house now relocated in Letchworth State Park. If a rod is a bit over 16 feet, as I seem to recall, Major Van Campen had some 160 yards to sprint between two long rows of unhappy Indians, running for his life, running for the council house on the riverbank—and across the river, if he could, to the future site of Houghton College. The tablet seems to imply that he made it. What wounds he received, and whether he survived them, it does not say.

The tablet in the boulder and its sunlit vision increase the feeling of historical evanescence that came to me upon seeing the disembodied head of Fancher Hall, floating in the trees like the torn face of Orpheus. One moment, a bloodied soldier of the Revolution, running for his life between 160 yards of Seneca Indians. The next moment, an untried pacifist from Oregon, lecturing on the Senecan roots of Shakespearean tragedy to long rows of Anglo-Saxons, uprooted Africans, and native Koreans in a riverstone classroom. How did we get from there to here, two hundred years later and just across the river, just across the river of time?

I recross the river on what I think is the Lattice Bridge, the one the road is named after. This bridge is floored not with steel grating but with tightly fitted planks. The tires on my bicycle go quiet as they pass from gravel to wood, then hum as they ease onto asphalt beyond. What seems to be a family gathering lies ahead in the shade next to an old house. A grizzled man hugs a hesitant girl (niece? granddaughter?) and whirls her around before she pulls away.

As I pass the house, four brown dogs speed from the yard, yapping, snapping, baring their teeth. One set of dogs before Major Van Campen, one set after him. My own gauntlet. A tubby fellow chases after the dogs, yelling, cursing. Three turn back, but one dodges into a cornfield and only pretends to give up the chase. He is keeping pace with me just behind the first row. My calf, to him, looks sweet, tender, a succulent ear of boiled corn. He sees his chance, darts back onto the road, but the fat man, out of breath, spots the dog and sends a rock skipping down the pavement after him. The rock shoots past the dog, whizzes just behind my back, and tears into the cornstalks.

The dog stops and I pedal on, back to Route 19 and south to the village, my village, to council houses of riverstone. I return again for a third year—wounded, exhilarated, a bit scared—with no bronze tablet along the road to hint whether I shall keep or lose my life in this place.

A Wilderness Journal

Day 1: Weather and Wordsworth

AS RAINDROPS GUST and spatter the canyon, I begin to wish I had brought a tent. Think of all the weight you're saving, I tell myself. Think of how wet you'll get, I reply.

I quicken my pace through alder groves, rock-hopping small pools and falls until I arrive at Manzana Narrows, my stop for the night. Like most camps in the San Rafael Wilderness, this one includes a somewhat crippled picnic table—an inviting place to sit and read, but not in the rain. I uncoil my bag beneath the shelter of a sycamore tree and crawl inside to the echoes of thunder. I'll save my volume of Wordsworth for later.

Still, I am happy to be here. From what I have read during lunch in the sagebrush along the trail, I recall Wordsworth celebrating his release from "City's walls," from "The heavy weight of many a weary day / Not mine," from "the burthen of my own unnatural self" as he returns to the Lake District of his youth. I've not been before to the San Rafael, this transverse sprawl of mountains on the central coast of California, so I can't exactly say I'm returning. But I am glad to be back on the West Coast after three years in New York, and glad to have a teaching job in Santa Barbara. And after my first year in the classroom at Westmont College, I feel again a release from the burden of my teacherly self, the joy of return to elemental nature. I have been looking at the edge of these wilds all year from campus and am curious to see what is here. From my starting point near Figueroa Mountain, I hope to ramble seventy miles to the Santa Ynez River and emerge renewed. What Wordsworth calls a "pleasant loitering journey."

The clouds thin as evening darkens, and I walk to the edge of a fall-fed pool some five feet deep. Beneath raindrops on the water's surface, a small trout quivers.

Day 2: A Note to the Forest Service

At dawn I climb cold winds to the aptly named Hurricane Deck. Behind me rises San Rafael Mountain, the namesake peak for the wilderness, sugared with snow from yesterday's storm. Odd: a few days and miles ago and away, I was sweltering through graduation at the foot of Montecito Peak.

From the top of the bare sandstone Deck, I look down into the vast reaches of the Sisquoc River. It expands my soul but also strikes a bit of fear. I don't know if I want to be alone down there. As I descend, the plot and the heat and the poison oak thicken—the trail does not seem so well traveled anymore.

On the bank of the river (a modest stream, in this drought year) stands a weathered guard station. The register speaks of thousands of ticks and a recently killed four-foot rattlesnake. "Note to Forest Service," it says: "Please stock larger rattlesnakes."

Upriver I stop at a snug little camp in a small grove of cottonwood, leaves dancing high in the evening air. Three sweaty horsemen clatter through, bound from Santa Maria to Ojai to celebrate the centennial of their alma mater, Thacher School. They have been on the river for two days and thirty hard miles, and look at me as if I am strange for being here alone and on foot.

Day 3: Avoiding the Lakers

Rattlesnakes. Crossing and recrossing the Sisquoc all day on a sometimes brushy trail, I am constantly checking the ground at my feet. One large serpent slithers through a bush beside me—at eye level.

Okay. So I have this phobia. I don't think much about bears, though notes in the register report sightings of several on the Sisquoc. I don't fear getting lost or meeting up with Flannery O'Connor's Misfit. Heights don't bother me—my favorite parts of the Sisquoc trail are the narrow ledges on canyon walls. But show me a snake, even a "nice" one, and I'll show you the whites of my eyes.

What would Freud say? (I don't want to know.) What was Eve attracted by? (Let Freud answer that.) I just know that that armless, legless coil and slither repulses me, and when I think of fangs, poison, and slow, agonizing death on the trail, it's almost enough to make me want to stay home and watch the Lakers in the playoffs with my shamelessly unadventurous colleagues.

But not quite. By day's end I switchback out of the Sisquoc past soothing falls and giant old growth: spruce, pine, cedar, fir. I make camp in what could be a Sierra grove. Across the trail is a grassy meadow and a cold mossy spring. I watch the evening bathe the valley below and repeat like a mantra, "Earth has not any thing to show more fair," those splendid words that Wordsworth wasted on the City of London.

Day 4: A Woman with a Past

Uptrail through more incredibly huge trees to another spring—and an ancient stove, sculpted out of cement and iron. It bears the date July 4, 1939, and lists five names, only one of which remains in full. (I write the name from memory tonight as Mary Hutchinson—but I must be mistaken. Mary Hutchinson is the name of the wife of William Wordsworth, and that would be too much of a coincidence.)

I think of her as I hike onward through steep oak woods, the trail padded with tiny gold leaves. I imagine her young, carefree, enjoying moments of mountain freedom even in the midst of the Great Depression and on the eve of a terrible war. As I climb to the top of Big Pine Mountain, I can think of no reason I should not meet this woman calmly seated on the summit, a sly half-century smile on her face.

What I do find there are traces of snow and farflung views along Mission Pine Ridge into rolling clouds. At Big Pine Spring just down the hill I warm myself at the fire of a quiet Irishman I first met on Manzana Creek at the outset of my journey. Ed is homeless, a devout Catholic who sleeps in the gardens behind the Santa Barbara Mission and attends mass every morning. It took him two days just to hitchhike to the trailhead, and morning and evening he eats little more than oatmeal. When he finds I am from Westmont College, he expresses his appreciation for a ride he once got in a moment of need with a Westmont group in Yosemite. As he describes the person who helped him, I recognize my brother Dave.

Fog soon envelops the evening, but after Ed crawls into his tent the moon appears, bright, gibbous. Below me the trees drop into an ocean of stars and clouds.

Day 5: Homelessness and Ancient Homes

This being Sunday, Ed asks if we might read Scripture and pray together before I leave. Though I do not know him well, his request does not strike me as awkward. He chooses John 15, "Love one another," and I Psalm 8, "O Lord, our Lord, how majestic is thy name in all the earth."

After we pray, Ed talks about his homelessness. Sometimes he thinks it is God's will, a call and way of ministry. Jesus was homeless: "Foxes have holes, and birds of the air have nests; but the Son of man has nowhere to lay his head." So were his parents in Bethlehem. God provides. I wonder if this is faith or inertia, but cannot judge. One thing emerges as certain: Ed resists any talk of finding a job.

I hike most of the day in dense fog on Mission Pine Ridge, so named because here the padres obtained the timber to build the Santa Barbara Mission late in the eighteenth century. I cannot imagine how difficult it must have been to haul those logs through miles of chaparral to the coast. I follow fresh bear tracks for the afternoon and take sudden interest in whistling and singing, especially near sharp rises and bends. Strange blobs of sandstone rise up in the blowing fog. I feel I am wandering another planet.

Mission Pine Spring, the first water for eleven miles, offers a pleasant but eerie camp beneath sugar pine and live oak. Hard-beaten earth and smooth-worn natural benches of stone tell years of use. I lie in my bag, listening to the trickle of water, and think of the padres, and the Chumash before them. They are said to have occupied Rincon Point, next to our home, for eight thousand

continuous years. I consider our tract house and wonder at our
pretensions to permanence.

Day 6: Something Far More Deeply Interfused

Today, the climax: a hike to the top of San Rafael Mountain.
From camp at dawn I overlook a bright floor of clouds from here
to the Pacific. They rise as I climb, and others form and descend
from above. On top I am almost caught in the sandwich. Entries
in the register report views from the Channel Islands to the Sierra,
but I swirl in giant columns of mist, onstage in the cloud drama.
Rain and wind catch me quite by surprise, and I sprint down the
trail to hide beneath the shelter of a rock.

I read quite a bit of Wordsworth's *Prelude* this afternoon, as I
have each day so far. It occurs to me I have never been to the Lake
District, much less the Lake District of the nineteenth century, and
that Wordsworth never hiked the chaparral ranges of California,
in his time or mine. But in my simple acts of reading and walking,
I have brought Wordsworth to myself, the Lake District to the San
Rafael, and the nineteenth century to the twentieth. My delight in
a cloud-wrapped mountaintop is Wordsworth's on Mt. Snowdon.
My communion with a homeless man is Wordsworth's with the
leech gatherer, the discharged soldier, and the myriad vagrants
of his day. Indeed, the very idea of hiking alone through wild
country as a way of cherishing the land is practically Wordworth's
own invention. When I think that I see with my own eyes, I am
using his.

Day 7: Bears and Snakes Recollected in Tranquillity

A woman named Kathy, a landscaper from Montecito, arrived
at the spring with her dog last night. This morning we talk. She
speaks wistfully of growing up on a farm in the San Joaquin

Valley, roaming the fields on long summer evenings and fishing for weeks in the Sierra.

Something of Wordsworth in this: a belief that growing up in nature can deepen one's imagination and fellow feeling. What I remember best and most of my own growing up are the woods and fields of Oregon. Like Wordsworth, I think a connection to a loved landscape has helped to give me what imagination, depth, and sympathy I may possess.

I think of my children, Jonathan (four) and Hanna (two), now growing up by a freeway. Lately, Jonathan's plea, morning and night, has been to go to Thrifty Drug and buy a toy. A store, not a spring, is the salient feature on his map. Being good parents, Sharon and I worry that in moving to the northern edge of southern California, we have deprived our children of one of the best parts of childhood. Sharon also grew up beneath the Sierra, where she would go on all-day rides through the foothills with her horse and dog. This may have something to do with why we fell in love and married.

But it is time to head downhill through hot chaparral toward Coche Creek, home, and Thrifty—in that order. My guidebook tells me that *coche* is Spanish for wild pig, some of which roamed here years ago. Bashing through thickets of poison oak beside the creek, I'm hoping they no longer do. But I am looking for snakes again, and before long, one obliges, rattling under a bush by the trail. As one of my new colleagues would say, "Oh, my heart!" I tiptoe around with lungs aflutter and creep down the path with eyes fixed on my vulnerable shins. After a few ridiculous minutes of this, I tell myself to look up once in a while in case, say, a bear appears.

I do, and one does. Brush snaps above the trail, and a bear indeed leaps onto the path, airborne for an improbable moment, then landing on all fours some thirty feet in front of me. Larger than a cub, and smaller, I think, than a full-grown adult, with golden fur on the back of its neck. It turns my way, takes one look at my gaping face, and eats me alive—no, plunges off in terror, actually. I laugh uncontrollably. Farce, of course—the stage business of an ursine about-face. But comedy as well, a happy ending, the opposite of Shakespeare's "Exit, pursued by a bear" in *The Winter's Tale*.

I emerge from these surprises into an open field of white wild oats, Flores Flat, an old homestead now unsteaded. The flat is bordered by spreading oaks, stately pleasure domes decreed by nature and my own willing imagination. Beneath one of these trees is a tall gaunt man from Bakersfield by the name of Stephen. It is his springtime ritual to camp here, as he did with his father back in the thirties. (I forget to ask if they knew "Mary Hutchinson.") In those days they came to hunt deer. Since then, he says, the brush has thickened appreciably and the deer have gone. He tells me about the bleeding ruins of two men who tried to descend a nearby trail that hadn't been cleared in twenty years. "Them poor bleeding suckers," he says and laughs like a donkey.

So we sit and talk in a leisurely way, as people do when meeting by chance in a wilderness roamed by solitary sorts. He is the eighth person I have seen in seven days. We are a small community, spread out in a vast place. That is the way we like it, and that is the way we like each other. "Love of Nature Leading to Love of Mankind," as Wordsworth puts it in one of his more didactic titles. I'll have the next camp all to myself. Stephen tells me this with the assurance of sharing good news.

A mile later I crest a larger set of fields (*potreros,* they're called), falling off in the evening light to the secret laps of sycamore. A warm wind blows, and I sit down in the waving oats to watch the mountains darken around me. Stephen showed me the place on Flores Flat where Carlos Flores had raised his cabin and built a flume, but there was no trace of them now. They are long gone. For now, it is just I, and the wind, and fields and fields of white wild oats.

I camp beside Santa Cruz Creek, in a hollow beneath huge oaks, interwoven, arch within arch. Alone at my table, writing by candlelight, I think I hear voices—in the wind, the water, the leaves, the crickets. Why do I hear them? Because I want to, or because I am afraid to?

Day 8: The End of Our Exploring

Switchbacking out of camp, I watch an arm of coastal fog reach into the canyon below and envelop the hills in a golden glow of morning light. I stop to write a sonnet in the enthusiastic manner of Wordsworth and think, yes, this might be a good summer to learn to write poetry. By the time I reach the shoulder of Little Pine Mountain, however, the romance is gone, replaced by flies and scorching heat. These I can leave.

At the Oso Creek trailhead I hear the voices—the real voices—of those I love most. I tell them, eventually, about the bear. Soon Hanna is acting out the dread encounter on all fours. Jonathan asks what its eyes looked like. An important question, now that I think about it: the clue to the character of that bear—who he was and how he saw me.

Driving us home, Sharon surprises a writhing snake on Paradise Road. It swirls like a dream on the asphalt glare, slips untouched between the wheels, and slowly disappears in the mirror.

Day 9: A New Love for Humankind

Today I drive with Jonathan to a rundown barbershop in the old part of town. I had my hair cut here a few months back by a young, friendly surfer named Marty, the son of the man who runs the shop, who is also named Marty. When I enter this time, an old fat fellow is slumped asleep in a chair in front of a television—Marty Senior. Marty Junior is nowhere to be seen. The man jumps up quickly, pretending he has not been napping, and greets us with energy. Jonathan begins to play with his trucks on the floor, and I seat myself in the chair.

"What will it be, young man?" he asks.

"Oh, about an inch off," I say.

"How much on the ears?"

"Leave a little there," I tell him. "A little over the top of the ears. And take just a half inch off the beard."

Marty Senior has a broad tan face and a very short crewcut. When he finds that I teach at Westmont, he takes a big step back. "They let you teach at Westmont College looking like this?"

"Like what?" I ask.

"Your long hair, your beard," he says. Apparently he is not joking.

"I guess I never thought of them as that long," I explain.

He changes the topic and carries on in a happy, expansive kind of way, switchbacking through many subjects as my eyes gradually close, taking up Marty's siesta where he left off.

I perk up just a little when he begins to speak about Marty Junior, how Marty should go to acting school. "Not to learn how to act in the movies," he says, pointing to the fifties musical on the TV screen, "but to learn how to act towards other people. To acknowledge and interact with them. A little normal give-and-take, you know?

"Some people," he says, dramatically stepping back from me, comb and scissors raised in the air—"some people just live inside their heads, you know what I mean? Like really, look at us here," he continues, looking at me here in particular. "We've been here together for twenty minutes, and are we really having a conversation?" He is beginning to sound angry. "Look who's holding up the conversation. I'm thinking to myself, why doesn't this guy talk to me? What's with this guy, see?"

Marty Senior pauses here, in case I would like to reply.

"Well," I say, softly and slowly, "I'm pretty tired, I guess. I just went on a long hike."

"Oh, of course," he says jovially, as if this solves everything. To my relief he returns to the chair and begins cutting my hair again.

I could dismiss what Marty has said as an unwarranted insult. But I think of a story by Flannery O'Connor in which a self-satisfied woman comes to a doctor's office, only to be attacked by a stranger in the waiting room who tells her she is a "warthog from hell." As it turns out, that is a prophetic word. So, I think, feeling the scissors go to work around my ears, do I live inside my own head to the exclusion of other people? How many people do I make as uncomfortable as I am making Marty Senior? Something I noticed on my hike was that life did not seem terribly different from being at school or at home. Do I live within myself so entirely that the presence or absence of others makes little difference? Am I always socially absent?

One way to answer these questions is to take refuge in my tested identity as an introvert. The man who gave me the Myers-

Briggs examination told me that introverts account for only a quarter of the people in America. The rest are raging extroverts. Two nations, two worlds, colliding in a barbershop.

Another way to answer these questions is to say, yes, I am an introvert, but sometimes I may have a responsibility to try to meet the extroverts of this world part way. So maybe I should wake up and talk to this guy, who has been suspiciously quiet the last few minutes. By the time I reach this conclusion, however, Marty Senior has finished the job.

"Take a look in the mirror," he says.

I put on my glasses and instantly see that Marty has done his small part for social reform. My beard is a patch of red stubble on my chin, and Jonathan could drive one of his trucks between the tops of my ears and my new trimline.

I am very silent.

"Well, well," he says, laughing. He is once again his backslapping self. "Hair—it always grows back, you know. That's what I always say. A little give-and-take never hurt anybody."

To Be in England

Only by going alone in silence, without baggage,
can one truly get into the heart of the wilderness.
All other travel is mere dust and hotels
and baggage and chatter.

—John Muir, *The Life and Letters of John Muir*

IT IS A TRUTH universally acknowledged that professors of English like nothing better than their trips to the British Isles (unless perhaps it is talking about their trips to the British Isles). But when it came my turn, as part of a cozy English Department in Santa Barbara, to accompany our majors for an autumn term in the land of our chosen literature, I felt only dread.

It was not that I feared sharing myself out of the classroom with my students. I had worked in the summers for many years as a mountain guide in the Cascades and Sierra Nevada and knew the rhythms of around-the-clock group living. But I also knew how wedded my well-being was to the vastness of the forests and mountains of the West. Four years of college near Chicago and three years of teaching in western New York had both been times of displacement for me. Wallace Stegner, in his book *The American West as Living Space*, identifies how necessary the nearness of the wild is to the mental health of Westerners. He calls our wilderness "the geography of hope."

I had never been to England before, but I was pretty sure it was not this kind of geography. A month or two before we left I expressed my foreboding in a poem, borrowing Stegner's memorable phrase for a title. Thomas Hardy got into it because I learned he had never been to America. Too bad for him, I thought. Maybe he would have been less gloomy if he'd taken the time to tramp around in the Cascades. Writing the poem was cathartic, I think, as writing a poem almost always is, but this pledge of allegiance to the West only set me up for a bout of depression, the worst I have ever experienced, once the semester in England began. I fulfilled my own prophecy.

The Geography of Hope

I have been in country that makes
my heart rise. On a black-hot ledge
by the Crooked River I saw it in the lilt
and shimmer of all Three Sisters
across the gorge. On a nunatak
in the Boundary Range I saw it
when the rose sun sank and the moon
climbed over the Taku. On the headwall
of the great Kahiltna I saw it in the gentle crest
of Hunter below, snow and cloud in conspiracy.

Even among the tangled chamise
of Montecito Peak I have seen it.

At times in my life I have lost
these places; I have seen the Rockies
recede in a rear-view mirror.
In the western suburbs of Chicago,
one house bows to another.
The land is gone, no one scans
the horizon. In the village of Houghton,
near Buffalo, there are hills, yes,
but nothing beyond their false promise.
They are foothills of no range of light.

And now, England.
I have been reading the elegiac
life and work of Thomas Hardy, who
though invited never came to America.
A shame, really. Had he washed
his cramped soul seven times in the Santiam,
he might have been cleansed of his epic gloom.
Perhaps it was only claustrophobia after all,
that European leprosy that has crept
across our continent five hundred years.

Wessex has its charms, I'm sure,
Houghton its woodlots, Wheaton its pride.
But just this: one night in western New York
I had a dream. I stood atop Cathedral Peak,
and the granite domes of Tuolumne
spread out at my feet like the beckoning
kingdoms of this world. The long white wall
of Sawtooth Ridge cut gleaming
across the far horizon, and lodgepole,
paintbrush filled the canyons in between.
I reached for them all, like Milton

for his espoused saint, and awoke,
sobbing, emptyhanded—the high home
place you have to be when cock crows.

For much of our time we stayed in a Tudor manor house called Hengrave Hall, outside Bury St. Edmunds in Suffolk. *We* included Sharon and our two small children, twenty-four students, and an untried teaching assistant. Hengrave Hall was built by a wealthy cloth merchant during the rule of Henry VIII. Today it is occupied and run as a retreat center by an order of nuns, and it has always been a Catholic household. Bloody Mary sought refuge here in the short reign of Lady Jane Grey, and Elizabeth came on royal progress to frighten the family into submission. We held class in the QE chamber, where she had supposedly slept, and a white bust of her majesty glowered down on us every day.

My teaching assistant, Laurie, slept in an absolutely gothic room dominated by a portrait of his Catholic majesty James II. Wherever you stood or sat in her room, the eyes of the deposed monarch followed you. The nuns told us the room was haunted, and one night Laurie was sure that something or someone stood by her bed.

Her story stuck in my mind, and late one evening I put aside my student papers to write a poem, "Hengrave Hall," about whatever it was that was haunting me. Brief and inarticulate as the poem may be, I think it represents an admission to myself that something was amiss with my mind. Trying to attend to my family, my students, and my teaching assistant—to be husband, father, teacher, mentor, and tour guide, all the while a stranger in a strange land—these things were wearing me out and wearing me down. The sustained intensity of this feeling was quite new. I was scared. And I still had two months to go.

Hengrave Hall

Midnight in the manor house, dark
rain hard against the leaded windows.
I trace the essays in my hands, words
finding words, the sound of poems
guttered into explications.

Last week my teaching assistant
felt a ghost approach her bed.
The moon was out, she heard
the footsteps, knew its presence
waiting beside her. An hour,
she said. She couldn't look.

The way I feel about papers tonight.
Except they don't scare me.
Not like I do.

Perhaps one month later, in early November, my family and I got away from the group for a weekend at Chepstow, at the mouth of the River Wye in Wales. But my dread and anxiety came with me. By now it had become noticeable to everyone that "something" was wrong. My affect in class was subdued, and students had stopped participating, choosing to hold their own discussions in the summer house of the manor. This added to my burden a crushing sense of failure. The American presidential election was just then at its climax, and George H. W. Bush was headed for strange and certain defeat. Though I am a Democrat, I felt a sense of identification with President Bush that fall and saw the surprised sadness in his patrician face on the television. One night I dreamed vividly of his stoic effort to conduct business as usual at a cabinet meeting in spite of his disappointment.

Wordsworth of course is a favorite of mine, and we had come to the banks of the Wye in part to revisit his haunts. One morning I hiked alone the five miles upriver in the fog to Tintern Abbey. Partway there, I stopped to write "A Few Miles Below Tintern Abbey," a poem with a title in stark contrast to "Lines Written a Few Miles Above Tintern Abbey." I realized in the poem that Wordsworth's epiphanies could not dispel my own depression. His experience was his, and mine was irrevocably mine. But even as he turns from the land at the end of his poem to rejoice in the presence of his sister, I realized I had a lifeline in the love of my own family. There is a desperate reaching for my wife, my children, at the end of the poem. At noon, I found them across the river. We spent the rest of the day together, above the abbey.

A Few Miles Below Tintern Abbey

I have no memory of this place except
in words. How often I have returned to them.
It is foggy now, early morning. Oak leaves
fall on my page, and the yew are dark,
dark and dripping. I sit above a bend in the Wye
over fields divided by woods and hedgerows—
even now I can hardly tell the difference between them.
There are gulls and squirrels beside me in motion
and cows below me that are not. And yes, in the fog
I could even say that the farmhouse at the top
of the pastures is green, green to the very door.

It is the fog that connects this scene. Things are not
nearly so clear as they were two hundred years ago.
The edges of vision are blurred now, the music
as sad and still as ever. At my back, in the cliff,
is a small gray cave. It might be wisest

to go there, to make full retreat from what lies
in wait at the end of the trail. Mossy ruins
are not enough. Another man's memories
not enough. I could be the curl of smoke
from the hermit's dwelling. I could die here.

But there is Dorothy to think about.
Perhaps it was only a compliment, but you did
say that if your sense of sublimity failed
on a given day, you would still find
comfort in those eyes, those wild lights.
Last night I shouted at my children
and sent them to bed without my blessing—
no little nameless act, that, but a desperate
disease of the soul. Eighty days in this land
together, and a souring of the eye and ear
and all that they create and know. But to see
the way they kissed me this morning,
their only love, and to hear the way
my Dorothy spoke to calm my fears as I left in the fog,
there was something there to linger on, something
deeply interfused, a thing far more deeply interfused
in my memory, and mine alone.

In that dark month of November, I had a recurring impulse
to beg total strangers for help. Chatting with a young Methodist
minister after services there in Chepstow, I clung to his brief,
polite friendliness and wanted to pour out my woes at his feet.
In Stratford, a veteran actor of the Royal Shakespeare Company
met with our group to talk one day about *The Taming of the
Shrew*. Hours later I saw him walking in the street. He looked so
wise, so caring, so keenly perceptive. I almost stopped him. But
what would I have said? *You seem like a good person to me. I am in
trouble!* At Hengrave, I did speak to a middle-aged priest while

we washed the community dishes one night. But he affected not to understand what I said. In Britain, perhaps, one does not talk about one's troubles.

On a trip to Oxford, we stopped at the Kilns, former home of C. S. Lewis. The morning was cold and rainy. A number of the students were in ill humor, wanting to be somewhere else, and refused to get off the coach. Some of us straggled inside, and one of the residents gave us a desultory tour. The place was dirty and disheveled, and much of the house was closed to us. But the old study, open at the end of the hall, had a certain presence about it. There were two desks set apart from the walls—one for "Jack" and the other for his brother Warnie. And on Jack's desk, to my surprise, was an old black rotary telephone. I picked up the receiver. "Hello?" I said jokingly. But I knew what I wanted. I wanted the voice of C. S. Lewis to comfort me. I wanted him to say that I would be okay.

Somehow, I made it to December and our plane home. On the flight, I sat next to a rumpled man who asked why I had come to England. "I am a college English professor," I said in a feeble attempt to impress myself by impressing him. "And I have been touring and lecturing with twenty-four students from California. For four months."

"Oh!" said the man graciously. "So you're a teacher! I'm a teacher too. At Oxford."

When we arrived home, there were welcome banners strung across our living room. Rather perversely, I tore them down right away. Was it because I didn't think I deserved to be welcomed? Was it possible that I could not even welcome myself? Is that what it means to be depressed?

Return

A fistful of calendar pages.
Back at my desk, I hold them in air,

a flimsy sheaf, all that remains
of an autumn in England.

So easily torn to update the past. See,
I release them. I throw away

four months of my life. They are gone now.
Who is it that held them, who is here?

A week after returning home to California, I hiked down Manzana Creek in the San Rafael Wilderness and found some unexpected solace. The smallest acts made me feel a little better about myself. I remember thinking, *I can cross a stream. Read a map. Pitch a tent. Fire up a campstove. I know how to do these things. I am an able human being.*

Seven miles downstream, where the Manzana joins the larger Sisquoc River, I came upon a one-room schoolhouse, a historic structure maintained by the county. It sat on a bluff in the wind beneath gray pine, a ghostly reminder of a hardy group from Kansas who had tried to homestead here in the late nineteenth century. According to my guidebook, they were led by a self-appointed patriarch with the unlikely name of Hiram Preserved Wheat. He was an illiterate faith healer who preached, among other things, the salutary effects of cooking with coconut oil. Some twenty families tried to make a go of it and miserably failed. Drought, flood, fire, poor soil, and sheer distance from market overcame them. The schoolhouse closed its doors for good in 1902.

Manzana Schoolhouse

At the confluence the creek is dry,
the river is dry. I see far
on its sandy road, the people,
the homesteads, the faith healer,
all the hopes held stubbornly
like sycamore leaves in dry December,
rattling gold until they drop
like fallen birds, like quail
who leave their lives in air.

The wind is here, and a warped
wood schoolhouse. Children came
for miles in summer, crossing
and recrossing streams
in live oak canyons, only
to learn they could not stay, that finally
we are visitors, that this land
had to be left untrammeled,
marked and settled in memory.

As I sat beside the schoolhouse, I thought how disappointing
the death of his dream must have been for Hiram Preserved
Wheat. He must have tried to convince his followers and himself
that they were in the promised land, only to have it dawn on them
that they were still in the wilderness. I wondered if his fifteen
years of struggle had left him as deeply discouraged as I was. (As
I write this now, the comparison sounds ludicrous. But it makes
me realize that, among other things, depression is an unwitting
form of narcissism.) The empty schoolhouse seemed to me a
metaphor of my own hollow experience as a teacher in England.
Sitting there, I felt an impulse to honor the dead who had failed

in other ways before me, these pioneers who likewise may have doubted their own competence and sanity.

The next day I scrambled narrow canyons to a huge cube of rock below Hurricane Deck that was sacred to the Chumash. At the foot of the rock were chipped and faded pictographs of condors, snakes, and centipedes in red and black and white pigments. After hesitating briefly, I climbed up a long ladder of hand- and footholds dished into the sandstone. On top were several improbably large pine trees and a natural pool of clear water, some four feet deep in a clean basin. I stripped off my clothes and immersed myself, then sat on the edge to dry in the mild warmth of the winter solstice, gazing out on the lonely expanse of the San Rafael Wilderness. It has never looked so good to me.

THE HILLS

The pastures of the wilderness drip,
the hills gird themselves with joy . . .

—Psalm 65:12

SWAGS:
The Next Generation

AS REUNIONS GO, we realized ours was suddenly in a family way. For countless summers most of us had guided trips in the backcountry of northern Yosemite. Sierra Treks was the moniker—Treks for short—and our Treks seasons had made us into friends for life. Until, that is, we started our drift into adulthood, and somehow became nurses and doctors and entrepreneurs and professors and wilderness activists. And parents.

That's what came home to us one Labor Day weekend on our annual SWAGS get-together at the horse camp in Tuolumne Meadows. (SWAGS stands for the School of Western Alpinism Guide School—a fictive but genuine para-Treks organization synonymous with our finest moments, e.g., bagging the wrong peak on a recon, enjoying another lightning storm from the security of a Sierra summit, rappelling off the end of the rope.)

SWAGS at the horse camp was a tradition. Only one of us owns horses, actually—my brother Dave, who left feet and hands on Mt. McKinley a long time ago now and has to get around by hoof. But even he comes mainly to climb—which he still can and does—and the horses are just to get us all admitted into the campground. (On Labor Day it's pretty crowded in the Meadows.) This year, however, the horses were busy most of the time giving rides to our many children.

Which can get boring after a while. Walking around the campground loop with halter in hand is good for only so long. After all, there's a trail that beckons a short two miles to Elizabeth Lake, and above the lake there's a cute little peak, right? Unicorn? Just a steep scramble at the top, isn't it? Something the kids might really enjoy.

So we talked ourselves into it—promising of course that at any point we could turn back—and pretty soon we were three families, a pair of horses, my brother Dave, and a couple of very sacrificially minded friends. Others, of course, went off to do some "real" climbing. How wrong they were.

After a SWAGS alpine start, something around 10:30 a.m., we made the two-mile hike to the lake without much in the way of footdragging. There was a boulder to climb along the way, and once on top you could throw marmot dung down at the others. (*SWAGS Reporter:* "Why did you climb Mt. Everest?" *Sir Edmund Hillary:* "So I could toss Yeti poop on everyone else from the summit.") The lake itself held an island boulder which also had to be swum to and conquered for lunch. But no marmot dung on top, a disappointment that threatened to erode morale were it not for a timely box of Cracker Jacks.

Early in the afternoon we turned our steps up the granite shoulder of the mountain. For a peak by the name of Unicorn, there seemed to be a lot of summits to choose from some fifteen hundred feet above us. But that decision hopefully would resolve itself as we approached. First we had to get there. As we ascended the broken slabs, the qualities of the members of our expedition began to emerge. The two eight-year-olds, Jonathan and Whitey, distinguished themselves by consistently choosing the hardest route available. Why trudge up a simple slab when vertical climbing is to be had? Nine-year-old Kate picked her way demurely behind, and her brother Clayton, just four, chose to ride on the shoulders of Sven, his more-than-generous stepfather. Which gave my daughter, Hanna, six, the distinct sense of her right to my own shoulders.

Halfway up we met my brother and his friend Faith, who had ridden there by some improbable and circuitous route. (Faith is a Methodist minister on the south side of Sacramento. She had just officiated at a funeral for a gang member, and partway through, she said, the girls in the gang had tried to pull the body from the casket.) Here the horses would be tied, and here we lost our first member. Kate and Clayton's brave mother, Kit, feeling weary, decided to call this niche on the shoulder her high point of ascent. Unwisely, she refused the offer of a novel to pass the time until we returned. The summit looked close, and we of course would be "right back."

Our diminished remnant pressed on, and of course the summit refused to be as near as it should. Only the timely intervention of M&M's and gummy bears, and the serendipitous discovery of a patch of snow in a shaded crevice, prevented breakdown and mutiny. Clayton wanted his mother; his elders, however, wanted the summit—for the children, of course.

The slabs gave way to patches of scree, and a trio of pinnacles at last loomed close above us. We made our way to a ledge beneath the one in the center and saw before us a narrow and exposed traverse to the true summit on our right. Serious men with ropes and helmets were descending the pitch with professional care, calling all the proper signals. ("Dang it, Herb—you put this nut in *way* too far again!") When they reached the bottom they took stock of our team and pronounced, "This summit is *not* for children."

"Oh yeah?" said Whitey. "I can climb 5.8, you know."

The handful of men to match this mountain remained unamused. Their problem was, if we could climb it, they would have nothing to brag about. It's hard to see your whole day wasted like that. They bid us an ominous farewell and left us to our foolhardiness.

We broke out a rope and a handful of slings and harnesses, and Whitey's father, Jim Percy, led the pitch to the summit block. I say Jim Percy since that is his full name and suggests his actual descent from the English Percies heroically featured in Shakespeare's history plays. (Remember Hotspur, in *Henry IV, Part 1*?) To look at Jim makes me want to believe in the reality of noble blood. Part nurse, part cowboy, part climber, he carries himself with a strength and poise in whatever he does. No wonder his son climbs 5.8 in the third grade.

Not that any of us really wants to push our children up or off the high cliffs. Recently, Sharon and I had taken our kids climbing for the first time down in Yosemite Valley. I set a belay halfway up an easy niche in the Church Bowl, and Hanna and Jonathan gamely tried to negotiate the well-worn rock. Jonathan finally managed to make it, knees and elbows wildly flailing and eyes glued to his wristwatch (since, he said, he was timing himself). Fifteen years before, I had witnessed a father urging his son up the same pitch without a rope from above. "I want to go swimming, Daddy," the boy had whined. "Son, I know you can do it," said the man. What a jerk.

Jim called back that the rope was fixed across the traverse, and he retreated partway to assist at a high step. We asked him what the pitch was like, and he told us it was "interesting." Yes, we thought, but will it hold the attention of a four-year-old? We sent Loie next to test our theory. She's actually forty or so, not four, but our kids get along with her best so we trusted her to report back more accurately. In her adult life, Loie teaches social ethics at the University of San Francisco. Right now she was supposed to be speaking at a peace conference in South Africa at the invitation of Nelson Mandela, but the peace conference had been called off on account of violence. So she was here, our unofficial good-times nanny. She tied into the line with a sliding safety knot—a prusik—and set off briskly, hesitating on just a few moves and saying things like "Whoa, Mama, this is *something*." When she got to the summit she struck her trademark cheerleader pose and laughed down at us nervously. This was not encouraging.

It was decided that Jonathan and I would go next. I climbed just below him, helping him with his trailing prusik. We went up a crack and then past a corner into sudden and serious exposure. From our narrow ledge, it looked as if we could swan dive into Budd Lake, many hundreds of feet below. I looked fondly across the lake basin to the southeast buttress of Cathedral Peak, which Sharon and I had climbed on our honeymoon years ago. Awash with nostalgia, I was thinking how much I liked the idea of family and mountains. "Daddy, that's a long way down," said Jonathan. He was quivering. "I'm really scared." I put my hand on his shoulder and said, "We're going to be okay, pal. I know you can do it."

What a jerk.

Our route swung up to the very crest and now became double-exposed, dropping off in two equally fearsome ways. But for some reason my son believed my assurances of safety, the sort I had offered nonchalantly to a generation of other people's sons and daughters. (Now I wondered if all these years I had really been lying.) So we made it to the bottom of an overhanging nine-foot block, where Jim was positioned to help us. I boosted Jonathan up into his waiting hands and then found a way to negotiate the step on my own. According to our guidebook writer, the route was only class 3 in difficulty. Perhaps after the climb we could have him arrested for child abuse?

Once over the block, Jonathan attacked the final scramble with increased confidence and not a little bit of pride. Loie welcomed us to the summit and clipped him to a loop of rope anchored next to the register, in which Jonathan took an immediate interest. To write your name and better yet to draw a picture on top of a mountain were pleasures he had never conceived of. He was even more delighted to find two pieces of candy that someone had left in the tube—a sort of alpine trick or treat. I felt a huge relief, a giddiness. A real summit with my son.

I positioned myself to watch and help and photograph the others as they ascended in pairs. Jim brought Whitey up, and Deb Percy, the funniest woman in America (okay, Yosemite maybe), came up with Kate. Both kids were just as shaky as Jonathan had been. "What's the matter?" he called down. "You scared or something?" Sharon accompanied Hanna to the point at which the exposure began. "I want to go down!" Hanna said. I looked at Sharon and we both nodded. Here, at least, some sanity was setting in. Hanna returned to the bottom with Faith, who prefers the perils of gang violence to roped climbing.

But sanity was not going to carry the day. Here came Sven up the rope, with Clayton strapped awkwardly across his chest in a tight harness. ("My penis!" cried Clayton. "What about your penis?" said Sven. "My penis hurts!") Sven is the inventor of Clif Bars, created in his Oakland bakery. He always brought us lots of them, and we helped him concoct advertisements to combat his evil rivals, the Power Bar people. One of his latest, in the *Utne Reader*, of which we were all justly proud, touted Clif Bars as the only truly postmodern energy bar on the market. To get Clayton up the mountain, however, Sven would need all the postmodern energy he could get. Like Jim, Sven was always supremely confident and competent on a hard climb. But not now. When Sven reached the nine-foot block, I saw him look rather worried for perhaps the first time in my life. When marrying a woman, it is not good strategy to drop her four-year-old son off a peak. As for Clayton, he was alternating bouts of screaming terror with calm reflection on his favorite breakfast cereals. Somehow they got over the block and onto the summit. Dave followed, pawing the rock offhandedly (as he likes to say), and everyone who was going to be was suddenly there.

We took many pictures, of course, and recorded the ages of one and all in the register, and the kids drove Loie wild by pretending to unclip from the anchor. In the mottled sun of late afternoon I looked out across the Meadows to Sawtooth Ridge on the north horizon. In a few years the children would be there too, deep into

Whitney at Forty:
An Alzheimer's Expedition

I WAS TURNING FORTY, and the east face of Mt. Whitney beckoned—a classic and adventurous route up the highest peak in the Sierra. We do these things. Our friend Julie had taken folks up the pinnacle of the Lost Arrow in Yosemite Valley on her fortieth birthday—a party of sorts. And she was willing to come along this time. So was Slick, another longtime partner of ours. But this wasn't going to be a party. A grudge match was more like it.

Two years before, in mid-September, Sharon and I had made the approach up the North Fork of Lone Pine Creek to the barren hollow of Iceberg Lake. We had arrived midday, and the face swirled in and out of cold gray cloud. To save weight for the next morning we scrambled several hundred feet to the foot of the route and cached all our climbing gear. From there we saw the sloping ramp of the Tower Traverse disappear into moiling fog above an abyss. It was eerily quiet, and that most emphatically included my wife.

That evening the clouds lifted to summit level, and we watched a local hotshot climb the face unroped in an hour and a half. He returned just at dark, when the clouds came down again and began to snow. We had only bivouac sacks to put around our sleeping bags—no tent—and our dawn start turned into a shivering thaw in the morning sun. The face was dusted white above us, but it seemed to be melting fast. It was Sunday—there were others there to climb as well—so at last we decided to take our chances.

But first we found we had only one rucksack between us. Given all we wanted to take in such conditions, it soon ballooned to anvil weight. And back up at the Tower Traverse, we discovered we were sixth in line: one party far ahead; two crossing ropes on a long, sloping part of the route called the Washboard; and two crowding across the traverse. Some of them were novice climbers, and all of them wore rock shoes. This last was of concern to Sharon, who felt ill-equipped in mountain boots. I was no help, of course, insisting that real mountaineers still wear boots in the mountains, just as we did in the seventies.

"This pack is really heavy," she said, changing the subject.

I checked my watch—it was 10 a.m., getting late. Someone started talking about the rockfall on the Giant Staircase, high on the route. "A bowling alley," he insisted.

Two guys with ropes slung over their shoulders came huffing up the approach behind us, fresh out of a Winston ad. "You waiting to do the face?" asked one, hoping we weren't.

I glanced at Sharon, who wore a look of special pleading. "No, just checking it out," I told them. "We're planning to do the class 3 route up the back."

Which we did. The ice and snow on the north face at the top of the Mountaineer's route, first climbed by John Muir, were nothing short of terrifying, but we joined the crowd of a hundred or so milling strangers on the tablelike summit and returned via a roundabout ridge. The next day we viewed the crowds on the summit again from the lonely top of nearby Mt. Russell and wondered at the strange attraction of name peaks.

Strange indeed. On Columbus Day—now two years later—Julie, Slick, Sharon, and I approached Iceberg Lake in the full moon of predawn. As sunrise came the granite peaks flushed nectarine. We broke thick ice on the lake to fill our bottles, then scrambled to the rope-up spot. It was mercifully empty. We had the east face to ourselves. The sun was up, the rock was warming—it was going to be a perfect day.

I set an anchor for the belay, pointed out the ramp to the others, and was just about to head out when a Forest Service helicopter emerged from nowhere and began to hover next to the face. The noise of the blades was loud and unsettling, ricocheting all around us like gunfire. No time to pause, however—we had a peak to climb—so concentrating on each foothold, I led out. Soon I had tiptoed forty feet across the face. The holds were getting decidedly smaller, the rock more decomposed. I could make an uncertain traverse to a thin corner farther left or attack a flaring crack above. (One route description had called this pitch "a wild waker-upper." At least.) I chose the crack. It looked as if I could wedge an anchor or two in there, and it had to be easier than it appeared—the traverse was rated just 5.3. After a couple of gymnastic 5.7 cranks, however, hanging on by one jammed fist, I knew the next move was even harder—too hard for my mountain boots. But, being the real mountaineer that I was, I scrapped and struggled a long time. No luck.

"I'm comin' down!" I shouted to Sharon, who was paying out the rope below me. The helicopter had disappeared. I reversed my moves in the flared crack and looked across the dicey traverse to the thin corner. Perhaps that was it.

"Why didn't you go up the ramp?" she shouted.

The ramp? I thought.

"The ramp you pointed out to us—you're way below it!"

I groaned. I retreated. Forty minutes had gone by. I stood in shame where I had started. "I can't believe it," was all I could say. "I can't believe it."

"That's okay," said everyone, trying to be nice. But it was October: the day would be short.

I reembarked on the real traverse and found it an almost hands-in-pockets affair. The climb unrolled slowly from there. We ascended in two rope teams, switching leads on the easy Washboard, escaping the cold alcove above to sunny terraces over a notch. Then we crossed the famous Fresh-Air Traverse, so named for the thousand feet of fresh air that suddenly opened at our feet. This part wasn't nearly as hard or scary as I had feared—in fact, it was pure delight. But that was the last we saw of the sun as it disappeared behind a buttress. My bones ached in the athletic chimney above, and the odd move on the gentler Giant Staircase took prodigious amounts of breath and strength and concentration.

This brought us to the Exit Crack, a 5.7 slot that was somewhat overhung. I flailed on the crux move halfway up, finding the sequence of holds but losing my balance each time—the walls kept pushing out on my rucksack. I lowered myself off a wedged stopper, dumped my pack, and thrashed to the top of the pitch—our eleventh. One by one I hauled up our four packs, then belayed everyone to a sandy alcove just above me. I was spent. Two leads of exhausting effort—one off route, and one most certainly on—had used me up. I had wanted to climb the east face of Mt. Whitney to prove to myself I was still young; I was finding merely that I was old.

We could not see the summit yet, but the walls above us had eased off considerably. It was getting late in the afternoon—the shadow we climbed in was deepening. Sharon and I had led the way so far, but now Slick headed up as a matter of course. I found I was grateful to watch him go—and Julie after—as if the weight of a second rucksack were suddenly released from my shoulders. Traversing the pitch behind them I felt calm and safe, knowing my friends had been here before. After that we trudged across a dusty shelf to the east buttress, then wound the spine of it three pitches through patches of ice. At each belay we looked out at the darkening land—the canyons below, the ragged profile of Lone Pine Peak, the dusk of the Alabama Hills, the wide flat of the Owens Valley. Each place stood for retrospect, our faded past.

We topped out in the warm light of sunset, not another soul on the summit. The whole Sierra was bathed in quiet. We were worried by reports of ice at the top of our descent route and needed to hurry. But first there was the matter of a few candles, stuck in the top of a Snickers bar. And then a gaudy Hallmark card, coyly presented. "Happy 40th Birthday," it read. "You're not over the hill yet . . . but from where you are, you should have an excellent view."

On Being and
Becoming a Mountaineer

From garden to garden, ridge to ridge, I drifted enchanted, . . .
gazing afar over domes and peaks, lakes and woods, and the billowy
glaciated fields. . . . In the midst of such beauty, pierced with its rays,
one's body is all one tingling palate. Who wouldn't be a mountaineer!

—John Muir, *My First Summer in the Sierra*

FOR SOME DARK DEED in my distant past, it has been my particular penance to serve time as the chair of a department of English. Last fall our new provost asked me the question I most dreaded: "What is your vision for the department?" I tried to excuse myself by saying that George H. W. Bush and I had a little something in common—namely, we did not get this vision thing. But the provost was persistent, so after thinking the matter over for about six months I reported back that I did have a vision after all, and that it was: To Build a Bridge to the Nineteenth Century. The provost found this hugely entertaining, but I found myself explaining that I really meant it. What we need to do, I said, is encourage the habits of leisurely attention that make the reading of literature both possible and pleasurable. The way to do that, I said, is to model lives of unhurried focus. Eschew the media, linger over meals, and saunter a lot between classes. Spend long afternoons waiting for trains while immersed in Wordsworth or Jane Austen. And if the trains don't come anymore, all the better. Railway stations—abandoned ones—ought to be the perfect place for poetry.

Which brings me to my favorite word, *mountaineer*. It sounds a little like *engineer*, which is what I first wanted to be when I grew up. And it is definitely a nineteenth-century word, both in its era of currency and in its connotations of a leisurely attention to landscape. Whether used by Sir Leslie Stephen or John Muir, the word *mountaineer* was not so much about assault and conquest as it was about a way of dwelling in delight. *From garden to garden, ridge to ridge, I drifted enchanted.* . . . But the word, I think, has fallen off the bridge somewhere between their century and our own. In our time the world and its peaks are full of climbers, but sorely lacking in mountaineers.

I would like to report that I meander squarely among the mountaineers of this present age, but that would be falsifying the data. Especially in my earliest years, growing up near the Cascades, I was wholly and purely summit bound. From the crater rim of the South Sister, our first triumph, my brother and I saw peak after volcanic peak rise northward into the distance. We made a pact to climb them all before the summer came to a close, and almost killed ourselves in trying. With a light heart and little more than a clothesline, we tempted fate on the Middle Sister, the North Sister, Mt. Washington, Three-Fingered Jack, and Mt. Jefferson on subsequent grueling weekends. The general idea was to arrive at a trailhead at dusk, hike in to a lake by flashlight, get up before dawn, and hurl ourselves at the nearest summit, bypassing any and all older climbers who chose to pause for the quaint purpose of tying themselves into a rope. We were very nearly obliterated by rockfall on Mt. Jefferson, so Mt. Hood, the highest and therefore holiest mountain of our state, had to wait until the spring.

I see now that we resembled nothing more than locomotive engineers. Locomotives do not exactly drift enchanted; they charge purposefully through the landscape down a prescribed track, imposing time on a timeless world. John Muir had unkind words for the tourist industry of his day which delivered whole trainloads of people at high speed against designated scenic targets. They could briefly disembark, dust themselves off, and declare that they had been there. I'm not sure we treated the Cascades any better.

My brother went off to college in Santa Barbara, where he climbed sandstone, and I to the suburbs of Chicago, where I climbed elevator shafts. In the summers we started to guide backcountry trips in Yosemite. The canyons and peaks of the northern part of the park began to work on us, the vast measureless calm of those Sierra days, but still there were the restless hormones of ambition that rushed us onward (something more and something less than the "glad animal movements" that Wordsworth recalls from his own "boyish days"). We felt it our duty to hike our charges past the point of exhaustion, and then to climb them well beyond the point of terror.

Ambition found its apogee in an expedition we formed one spring to Mt. McKinley. The coldest and highest summit on the continent would surely afford the ultimate chance to prove ourselves. Get to the top of *that* mountain, and we'd have bragging rights for a lifetime. It didn't work out that way. After three weeks of blizzard and cold, I found myself hallucinating, knees buckling, still eight hundred feet from the top. My brother had it a lot worse. Trying to care for another exhausted team member, he lost his hands and feet to frostbite. Theirs was an epic three-day struggle back down to our high camp.

This is the experience that made us into mountaineers. It didn't happen right away, but it may have started the day a copy of Steve Roper's new *Climber's Guide to the High Sierra* arrived at the Anchorage hospital. Looking through it, my brother said something like, "Why did I come to Alaska when I could be running around in shorts in the High Sierra, having fun?" I may not have been there at the time—I may have been back in the Sierra, dutifully hiking groups of trekkers into the ground. But sooner or later I heard about his saying this. It is one of the things about our tragedy that moved me, and one of the things I may have learned from.

My brother became a mountaineer when he got a horse. At first he used her to try to do climber things, things that horses shouldn't do, such as ascending granite slabs and steep snow. But after a while he got to where he liked just to poke around in the trees and meadows for days at a time and smoke cigars by the campfire. The primary sense of the word *mountaineer,* even in the nineteenth century, was "mountain climber." But the sixteenth-century sense of the word, found for example in Shakespeare, was the somewhat derogatory one of "mountain dweller" (as in "some villain mountaineers" or "Yield, rustic mountaineer," spoken by Cloten in *Cymbeline*). This is the sense that John Muir reinvents, changing local habitation into a positive quality of being, and this is the sense I am beginning to understand.

One of the more heartwrenching moments of John Krakauer's famous book on the 1996 Everest tragedy, *Into Thin Air*, describes the last night before the summit attempt. The group has staggered, one by one, onto the bleak wasteland of the South Col and disappeared into their tents. It becomes obvious to Krakauer that they aren't really a team at all, just an assortment of paying customers, united only tenuously by the fierce desire of their egos. The loneliness and terror of this realization surpasses even the terror of the storm that comes the next day to claim the lives of half the party. In that moment of vision, that glimpse into a moral abyss, Krakauer and his companions are pure climbers, mere climbers, people who have gained a mountain but lost their souls.

For some reason I want to contrast those lonely consumers shivering on the South Col with my own family and the family of an old friend, camped together last summer at a lake far from any trail in the northern part of Yosemite. We had brought a rope to attempt a commanding summit across the lake but settled for a small knoll because of the danger of thunderstorms. We chose to call it Elf Mountain, after the propensity of our daughters to see elves in every rock and flower and stream about them. Our youngest children led the way, choosing the most circuitous route imaginable. We sat on top and looked out on Tuolumne Meadows in the distance as long as we liked, then slid down the same snowslope several times until we felt like wading in a sandy pool trapped between a meadow and a long, sinuous granite slab. Toward lunchtime, we followed a tiny outlet stream down a series of cascades and columbines until we found our packs again and took up the serious business of having to get somewhere by dark. I am forty-one years old as I write this and have touched more than a few summits since first climbing the South Sister at the headstrong age of fourteen. But Elf Mountain may be the first peak I have wholly climbed as a mountaineer.

Gary Snyder says it gently in his poem "For the Children":

> stay together
> learn the flowers
> go light

And John Muir says it grandly:

> Climb the mountains and get their good tidings. Nature's peace
> will flow into you as sunshine flows into trees. The winds will
> blow their freshness into you, and the storms their energy,
> while cares will drop off like autumn leaves.

When Muir asks, "Who wouldn't be a mountaineer!" he is so sure of the answer that he substitutes an exclamation for a question mark. But the real answer to *Who wouldn't?* is most of us, most of the time. For the invitation is to both a narrow way and a pathless way. The gentlemanly Sir Edmund Hillary, returning from the summit of Everest, told his companions that he had "knocked the bastard off." But as someone else once said, someone who once beheld all the kingdoms of this world from a mountaintop, the way of the mountaineer is to enter the sacred not violently but as a child.

New Seeds in California:
The Contemplative Journals
of John Leax

SOME YEARS AGO, I stepped off a plane on a spring day in Rochester and was met by Jack and Linda Leax. Nearly done with graduate school on the West Coast, I had come to be interviewed for a position in the English Department at Houghton College. Jack's friend and colleague Lionel Basney had decided to teach at Calvin College, at least for a year, and someone needed to fill in. I have since thought that it must have been hard to receive a person hoping to take over the desk of your best friend, but Jack was fairly gracious about it.

He and Linda took me to a Mexican restaurant and did their best to put me at ease. What I liked most, however, was his own trace of nervousness. I sensed I was in the presence of a private man who cherished his few hours alone with ax or pen, Linda or

Lionel. So we had a little something in common. I would rather have been hiking in the Sierra Nevada, he would rather have been spading his garden, and we were both stuck in this crummy interview.

When I arrived with my family that summer, my wife and I read Jack's new book, *In Season and Out,* a journal of a year at Houghton. We hoped it would acquaint us with the community we were stepping into. In oblique ways, *In Season and Out* did inform us about the people and countryside of this small portion of western New York. But mostly the book was about Jack. Or about Jack watching himself watch his garden. For example, he writes:

> Bent over in the sun, I sweated through both my shirts . . .
> and picked a half bushel of green beans. An equal number of
> yellow beans awaits my attention tomorrow.

When he wasn't picking beans he was chopping wood, and we got to hear about all of it.

At the same time I was reading a manuscript a friend of mine, Chris Norment, had written, titled *In the North of Our Lives.* It was the journal of a sixteen-month canoe trip from the Yukon to Hudson Bay, with a ten-month winter stopover in the Arctic Barrens. There were unnamed mountains, harrowing rapids, and caribou that blackened the tundra in great herds. Jack's book, by comparison, seemed rather tame and claustrophobic.

Before Lionel Basney left town I told him of my two responses to these books. "Don't judge one by the other," he told me. "Each approaches our experience of nature in a different way: one is intensive, the other extensive." That gave me something to think about, and it made sense in an East-Coast/West-Coast, yin/yang sort of way. You have Henry Thoreau watching those tiny ants by his pond, and you have John Muir riding a winter avalanche in Yosemite and living to tell about it with glee. You have Jack Leax picking his beans in his backyard, and you have Gary Snyder running the ridges like a wolf. I knew I would probably always prefer the extensive experience of the mountains and deserts of the West, the place and feeling that Wallace Stegner has memorably called "the geography of hope." But I also realized I needed to learn about whatever this garden business was. John Muir regarded Thoreau as a man who could "see forests in orchards and patches of huckleberry brush." I'd always understood that as a well-framed insult. But now I wondered if it might also or even mostly be a compliment.

Three years at Houghton began to give me an appreciation for the steadiness and wisdom, the placedness, bound up in Jack's person and writing. I began to see how his patch of woods that he calls Remnant Acres was every bit as much a geography of hope for him as the farflung canyons of northern Yosemite were for me. And when I left with my family to take a job at Westmont College in Santa Barbara, great parts of us were sorry to go. Without knowing it, we had begun to establish our own sense of place in western New York. Part of this was Jack's doing.

At Westmont I began to assign *In Season and Out* to my writing students. Later on I gave them his second journal, *Standing Ground*. Each time, I have to confess, I expected my students not to like him. And each time I was wrong. In every one of a half-dozen courses, the students preferred Leax over anything else we read—and "anything else" often included many of the superb essays in Donald Hall's *A Writer's Reader*.

This puzzled me. Leax's prose is plain to the point of intentional drabness. The persona who inhabits this prose is a forty-some-year-old professor from a little town back East who seems to spend most of his time contemplating the depth of compost in his garden. My young students, by contrast, were southern California hip, committed creatures of the cinema, freeway, and shopping mall. Most of them, conditioned by an Orange County conservatism, could not hear the word *environmentalist* without mentally adding the prefix *radical*. They weren't much interested, they thought, in nature or in nature writing, intensive or extensive. Yet they liked Jack Leax's journals a lot.

I have come to think this liking is for three reasons—the first of which they are conscious of (the other two, less so). Most of my students, when asked what has surprised them about Leax's work, respond that they are taken aback by his honesty. By *honesty* I do not think they mean the sort of personal disclosure that provides subscriptions to *People* magazine. There is next to nothing in Leax's writing that one could describe as sensational. Rather, the sort of honesty my students respond to has to do with the ready admission of personal limits—limits of knowledge, control, and power. Let me illustrate.

In *Standing Ground*, as Leax thinks about those who would site a nuclear waste dump across the river from his home, he develops at length a theology of holy hatred. But near the end of the book he suddenly announces he may be wrong: "All I have written about holy hatred leaves me unconvinced." A reversal like that is absolutely stunning to students—and perhaps to evangelical students most of all. They know of course what it is like to change their minds, but they didn't know they could do it in public—least of all in print. Through this one kind of honesty, Leax reassures us that our answers to questions are tentative, that it is okay not to know, that the best we can do is try to know.

Another sort of honesty emerges in a passage like the following from *In Season and Out*:

> Today, for no reason I can discern, I've had a feeling I'm no longer the man known by my friends, that every conversation I begin is an effort to reestablish a common ground. Suddenly I'm afraid that I have to remake all my friends and that time is running out. . . . The risk involved seems so great I wonder if I can fake it.

These are the words of a man who is not feeling in control, who cannot claim an ironclad identity, who admits to the adolescent who still lives inside of him. Needless to say, my students and I, as we say in California, can relate.

Related to this limitation of control is an honesty that admits to a lack of power and success. In *Standing Ground*, Leax reflects upon two students he finds himself unable to help, one a freshman reluctant to write, the other a senior lacking basic skills. He says of the latter:

> I will probably struggle through the rest of the course suggesting things to her she cannot do, and I will fail her, just as I will fail the freshman who hates to write. Make no mistake, both students will pass; I, the teacher, will fail as I almost always do.

This passage produced a moment of truth in my own classroom. "I can't believe this!" sputtered a student in the back. He was the star pitcher on the baseball team. "Do you feel like this?" he demanded. "Do you feel like a failure as a teacher?" Everyone grew uncomfortably quiet, including a guest faculty member who was sitting in for my tenure review.

I looked our pitcher in the eye and said, "Most of the time. Most of the time I feel like a failure as a teacher. Except for right now."

So, as I see it, my students like Leax because he tells the truth about his limits of knowledge, control, and power. They are so surprised by this that it makes me wonder about the level of dishonesty they must take for granted in the evangelical rhetoric available to them in churches, chapels, Christian media, and what goes by the name of Christian literature. It makes me wonder what lies we tell to ourselves and about ourselves, and what lies we encode as part of our official versions of the gospel. Leax at least admits to this entanglement and in *Standing Ground* reflects on the fictive nature of the truthtelling persona in his journal. And it is well he does, for in real life, he is not always known to tell the truth. During that job interview some years ago, I naively asked him if there were any problems between the faculty and administration. He looked at me with a straight face and firmly pronounced, "Absolutely none."

In any case, this so-called truthtelling lays the basis for a second reason that my students like his writing. And it is this: quite often they come to respect and advocate Leax's stance of care toward the creation. Given their adoration of Rush Limbaugh, this always comes as a shock to me. Further, you would think they could gain this sympathy from other environmental writers who are generously represented in Donald Hall's anthology.

Wendell Berry, for example, in "A Native Hill," also offers a creation-sensitive meditation in an Eastern rural setting, in prose that is more richly textured than Leax usually cares to attempt. But as much as I try to impress upon them the wisdom and beauty of Berry's essay, my students in general won't have it. They focus on the passages in which Berry objects to the stubborn otherworldliness of Bible-belt fundamentalism. He complains, for example, that

> such religion as has been openly practiced in this part of the world has promoted and fed upon a destructive schism between body and soul, heaven and earth. It has encouraged people to believe that the world is of no importance, and that their only obligation in it is to submit to certain churchly formulas in order to get to heaven. And so the people who might have been expected to care most selflessly for the world have had their minds turned elsewhere—to a pursuit of "salvation" that was really only another form of gluttony and self-love, the desire to perpetuate their own small lives beyond the life of the world.

"See," they say, "he hates Christians and worships nature." All of Berry's statements and allusions to the contrary are apparently invisible to them.

But with Leax it is different. They are sure he is a Christian as they think of themselves as Christians. And they have come to trust the honesty with which he relates his many struggles—struggles they recognize in themselves. So when he turns his thoughts to stewardship, to earthkeeping, they are ready to accompany him. One student who had taken offense at Wendell Berry was eager to point out a passage in *Standing Ground* in which Leax reflects on the environmental implications of the words of an evangelical hymn:

"And the things of earth will grow strangely dim in the light of His glory and grace." What irony! Oh, I know the intent of the words, the truth they reach after. But I know also their falseness, the abuse they have permitted, and the [opprobrium] they have brought on the church.

The student spoke as forcefully for Leax on this point as he had spoken against Berry on the same point a week or two earlier. He was unaware of any shift in his position.

So. My students like Leax's honesty, and that honesty woos them to begin to share his concern and care for God's creation. This concern and care, however, occur in a particular place that Leax takes great pains to define and to elaborate. This place is called home. It is my guess that this image and ideal of home that Leax provides in thorough detail is the deepest and unspoken reason my students are attracted to him. It may be that this more than anything bridges the gap of time and place and circumstance that separates Leax from this unlikely audience. For I suspect these southern California students are at some level aware of their essential transience. Home for them is a dreary succession of tract houses and often a more painful succession of blended families. Leax presents a stable, simple continuity of mother, father, and daughter living year after year in an old house in a small town, watching their garden come and go in season and out. He pictures relationships that grow and deepen in community over time, the way trees slowly thicken and take root. It turns my students green with envy. It is something they have not experienced. Or if they have experienced it, they have all too often felt it cut off brutally before its time.

Leax has much to say about this discipline of placedness, particularly in the opening pages of *In Season and Out*. He aspires to stay put, just as his literary mentors have learned to do before him: Henry David Thoreau, William Carlos Williams, Thomas Merton, Wendell Berry. He aspires to be as married to place as he is to his wife, and for one relationship to stand for and inhere in the other. He aspires to stay home as a way of resting in Christ:

> None of this is easy. But when I drive up to the house at 19 Torpey Street, I feel a sort of joy. I look at the massive white front rising nearly three stories above me. I look past the house to the trees I have planted. I look past them to the woodpile and to the garden. I hear the voices of my wife and daughter. I know all of this has come to me by grace that someday I might become a man worthy of what I have been given.

In just this way, Jack Leax and his work are a grace that has been given to my students and to me. We feel a joy as we approach his honesty, his care for the earth, and the homegrown nature of that care. His most recent book of prose, appropriately titled *Grace Is Where I Live: Writing as a Christian Vocation*, I am eager to bring to my students as well.

And where do I stand, you ask, apart from all this classroom business? I'm still out there with Gary Snyder, as extensive as ever, running the ridges like a wolf. I keep inviting Jack to join me, to climb the mountains and get their good tidings. But he won't come. Like that prissy friend of his, Henry Thoreau, he's afraid of heights. Besides that, he's waiting for me to grow up. And maybe I have started to. After a wonderful day of rockclimbing last week, I came home and planted a little wisp of a garden that might amount to a hill of beans.

Development Dreams

It was a miracle of rare device,
A sunny pleasure-dome with caves of ice!

—Samuel Taylor Coleridge, "Kubla Khan"

LAST NIGHT I DREAMED I was trapped inside a cave of ice in the Lemon Creek Glacier in southeast Alaska. No great surprise, since I once spent most of a month mapping this cave on the Juneau Icefield. I was just out of high school, tagging along with a group of glaciologists conducting research on this storm-soaked, spectacular roof of the Boundary Range.

The cave was half an hour's walk from our Quonset hut on a rocky ridge, which itself was a difficult hike from the sea through rainforest, up steep meadow, and over another crevassed glacier. This particular set of caves drained a lake that was pinned in a moat between the glacier and its headwall. One tunnel swirled down into echoing keyhole passages. Wearing crampons for purchase, we held our Coleman lanterns aloft and waded knee deep in the rapids until the rope and our courage played out—some 250 feet beneath the snowy glacier surface. Another tunnel extended horizontally, sculpted out of blue and white and replete with sudden waterfalls that roared from round holes in the ceiling and at other times and other places congealed into silent pillars, Inuit versions of Lot's wife.

It was the end of summer when the lake drained to expose these passages. Other students and researchers had moved on to other camps—it was just another boy and I who were left to explore the caves together. Being young, we were eager, determined, and easily awed. Many an evening we headed out into howling storms to make our way to the quiet sanctity of our cave for a night's work. We might emerge to a sky so filled with stars that the glacier glowed, a miracle of illumination.

But back to my dream, my nightmare. I was in the cave all right, but so were dozens of other people, cheerfully dressed in mitts and parkas like tourists on a cruise ship to Antarctica. The walls of the cave were lined with displays of the sort found in national park visitor centers, along with soda and candy machines. There was a video game or two, computers that spoke in genial voices, piped-in music, and bathrooms that were wheelchair accessible. In my dream I kept trying to find a way to the pristine parts of the cave, but each passage I tried was also lined with displays and machines, not to mention coffee cups squashed on the floor. People traipsed up and down the cave as I and many others have done at the Brontë parsonage in England—once a home, now a common thoroughfare. The Lemon Creek Glacier cave—once a frozen sanctuary, now well thawed by the fur-lined boots of the public. I awoke feeling violated.

I have had other visions of this sort. Once while camping in Slide Canyon in the Yosemite backcountry, I dreamed that a freeway and lodge filled the meadow and that the granite echoed with traffic. Again last summer, far from the road, along Piute Creek in the John Muir Wilderness, I dreamed the trail was now a highway, our campsite a spreading resort. Of course, these are not just dreams. John Muir could hardly imagine the present state of Tuolumne Meadows, with its sinuous line of automobiles insisting their way through the gleaming perfection of slabs and domes. And his worst nightmare, Hetch Hetchy, the damming of the Tuolumne River within a declared national park, came true and remains true for us today.

But sometimes it is the little invasions that break my heart. In the mountain canyon behind my home in Santa Barbara, a mile and a half of hiking and scrambling brings you to the foot of a seasonal waterfall. The water comes layering off in white folds for perhaps a hundred feet or so over bright orange sandstone. I had come for ten years to the base of this fall before someone showed me a clever system of ramps and cracks that led to the top. It took some skill and care, but the ledge on the brink in the shade of a spreading bay tree was a pleasant and a private place. From there you could look back down the canyon to the shore and across the channel to the islands, waiting in the outer sunlight. A little farther up the creek, somewhat trickier climbing brought you to the summit of a diamond-shaped pinnacle. Here the view was even better. I came here with the occasional companion who was up to the climb. We felt good there, away from others, somewhat proud of our efforts and the courage that in our minds had singled us out for such a place. Last month, however, I brought my wife and a friend here amidst many mock complaints that there had better be an easier way to get down. Unfortunately, there was. Gathered around the diamond-shaped pinnacle were no fewer than twenty people, all of whom had hiked up a newly brushed and constructed trail that circled around from the canyon below. I was mortified. The place apart was now just part of a common path. The inaccessible had just got accessed.

In graduate school I had a Marxist office mate who was wryly amused by my efforts with the Sierra Club to help preserve wilderness. "Americans," he said, "have a hang-up with virginity." Hmm, I thought. Did I have a hang-up because I liked wilderness, and because I liked it pristine and hard to get to? Was Aldo Leopold elitist to yearn for blank spots on the map? A more useful question then came to mind. Would Tuolumne Meadows be better treated—and better loved—if we had to walk there? Inaccessibility perhaps suits not only the few who make the effort to live in or journey to a given place on its own terms; it may also suit the place itself. The place is not virgin, of course, and never has been. In and of itself it is in free and constant intercourse with the entire universe, and its few human visitors or inhabitants are merely its conscious paramours. But the place that is difficult of access, while not virginal, is certainly and properly chaste. It is chaste in the sense that it is protected, as anyone or any place has a right to be, from gang rape.

Last month a friend and I hiked several days on an all-but-abandoned trail to an alpine lake in Kings Canyon National Park. As we scouted for campsites in the evening, I came across a quiet cove framed by hemlock and whitebark pine that looked out upon clouds and cliffs and waterfalls. Snowy peaks rose in a ring from terraces of distant meadow. Closer at hand, the grass around me formed a cozy amphitheater thickly planted with lupine, yarrow, aster, and paintbrush. Wordsworth once simply and profoundly said of a cottage girl, "Her beauty made me glad." That's how I felt. In fact, the presence of this place, grand and intimate at once, brought me suddenly to tears.

Then I turned and saw, to my surprise, a bronze plaque on a boulder behind me. It was a small memorial to the wife of an eminent California geologist. (No, I am not naming names.) I welcomed her memory there—the bronze plaque was no intrusion. I welcomed her brief association with this place before I was born, before even my parents were born. The lake, I saw, was named for her. That evening, we were her guests.

The next day a lone hiker told us that the geologist and his wife used to come to the lake quite often, long and difficult as the trip would have been at the turn of the century. One summer they even brought with them their three-year-old daughter. That, I thought, was fine with me. I could dream of nothing better.

EPILOGUES

The more words, the more vanity,
and what is man the better?

—Ecclesiastes 6:11

Do You Want Some Company?

I HAD PUT IN A LONG DAY at a writers conference in Palm Springs and returned to my hotel for the night. A Ramada Inn. Something in me does not like a hotel. I was staying here only because the closest Forest Service campground was over thirty miles away. In a hotel room I feel closed in a box, restless, uneasy. The Gideon Bible seems foreign to me, all those passages arranged for timely help for the traveler. And the television imposes itself, asking to be turned on. I do not normally watch TV, and when I do, I usually regret it. But I noticed that this one offered movies for a little extra charge, some of them adult movies. Of course, the better part of me did not want to watch these movies, knowing I would regret them even more than the normal fare. But still, there was that opportunity, should I decide to take it.

So I dropped off to a restless slumber, then a deeper and more peaceful one. Suddenly, I was awakened by a ring. The clock said it was 3:30 a.m. I leapt from the covers. I was thinking, *Family emergency*. I was thinking, *My wife, my children, my aging parents.*

I lifted the receiver. "Hello?" I said.

"Is this room 112?" said a woman. I assumed this was an operator, the person at the night desk.

"Yes," I said.

There was a slight pause. Then she said, as if it were the most natural and delightful question she could ask, "Would you like some company?"

Just like that. Her voice was full of music, fun, and innocence.

"No, thank you," I said politely and hung up.

I got back in bed, not quite believing what had just happened. What if I had said yes? She sounded like an interesting person. She sounded young and beautiful.

Then the phone rang again.

"Hello," I said.

"Hello there," she said knowingly. We were old friends by now. Obviously, she had counted on those second thoughts I had just been having.

"You know," I said, "I didn't call for anyone."

"I know," she said. It was as if she knew all kinds of things about me. "How old are you?"

When I told my son about this part of the conversation, he said I should have replied, "I'm eighty-two, and my toenail fungus is just starting to respond to treatment."

But I just said, "Good night." And hung up.

A good night for her, perhaps, but not for me. I lay awake in my bed till dawn. When I got over the oddity of it, and, to my shame, the undeniable temptation of it, I realized I was mainly feeling two things: fear and anger.

I had no idea how this woman knew I was alone in room 112. Was there a hotel clerk on the take, passing along room numbers? Or was someone registered as a guest, sipping drinks beside the pool and all the while taking note of who emerged from what door? The people in the room beside mine—by the sound of their voices an older man and two young women—packed up and left at 5:00 a.m. Suspicious, I thought.

The hotel manager, when I finally got hold of him a few days later, chalked it up to some high-school kid, making a prank call. "We are a three-star family resort," he said authoritatively. "Our employees are completely trustworthy. This kind of thing *does not* happen here."

"Well, it happened to me," I said, cleverly switching from deduction to induction. "And the person that called was poised and practiced. She knew exactly what she was doing. I think I'd like a partial refund."

The Chamber of Commerce was more sympathetic and gave me a complaint form to fill out. The police were upset that I had not called right away. My wife wants me to hold out for a full refund, which helps me feel reasonable about asking for only half of my money back. But the manager is sticking with his prank-call theory.

"Now you know how women feel most of the time," my wife says. And she may be right. This strange little experience, something that made such a good joke while I was chumming around with other writer guys at the conference, has made me feel sickeningly vulnerable. The voice of the woman on the phone simply will not fade away. It rests on the lips of chance women in magazines who are offering products presumably other than themselves. It wants to be recognized in a body, and wherever I look, it shape-shifts. It wants to keep reminding me, just like the Gideon Bible, that it is not good for a man to be alone.

Accidental Admissions

YESTERDAY I SAW AN ITEM in the paper about a man who was killed in a one-thousand-foot slide down the Peters Glacier on Mt. McKinley in Alaska. It caught my attention because, twenty-six years ago, I too slipped and fell in the same place, just below Denali Pass. Like the nameless man in the newspaper, I was descending; unlike him, I was roped to another climber. Don Wheeler, may he live forever, dug in his boots and his ice ax while I sailed, blissfully, headfirst on my back, toward rows of open, deep crevasses. The altitude had addled me more than it had addled him.

Being on a rope, however, is no guarantee of safety. The same short article in the newspaper also told of three brothers from Anchorage who perished together on nearby Mt. Foraker. They fell two thousand feet to their deaths, all on the same rope. I have never climbed Mt. Foraker, though I have stood at its base and contemplated its lovely, almost perfect form. But I do come from a family of three brothers.

"Just think how their parents must have felt," my son said when I told him about this accident. And I think now how my own parents must have felt when two of their sons, at age twenty and twenty-three, blithely left to climb Mt. McKinley. At the turn of the last century, a great-uncle of ours went to the Klondike and never returned. For him it was not Denali Pass but Chilkoot Pass that became the point of mortal reference. Unlike Uncle August, we did come back, though my older brother lost goodly portions of hands and feet to the mountain, and both of us lost our youthful pride.

This spring I applied for a new life insurance policy. The underwriter asked on the phone if I smoked (*no*), drank (*no*), had any of a number of diseases (*no*), and did I climb mountains? (*Well, yes. Sometimes.*) Then came a form in the mail on which to detail my increasingly meager exploits, and then the news: because of my "adocation [*sic*] of mountaineering," my annual premium would be not $460, as originally suggested, but $1,342.50. "Why did you tell them?" asked my wife. And indeed, the truth has never looked so costly. I e-mailed the company my protest with further explanation of my experience, competence, and safety—but all I got in reply was a second notice, asking for my balance of payment.

Now I see this item in the paper and think, well, maybe these orthographically challenged agents in New York City are right. Three brothers on one rope. A nameless man who slipped and fell where once but for the grace of God I might have not so gently gone into that icy night before him. And, truthfully, once I did ricochet two hundred feet down the sloping summit of Eagle Cap in the Wallowas of Eastern Oregon, equipped only with ski poles, and was saved by the merest chance of a snowbank perched atop the precipice of the north face. A stellar moment of experience, competence, and safety.

And speaking of Oregon, what about the foursome of climbers on Mt. Hood who, descending the summit, lost their purchase and swept the two rope teams below them into the only crevasse on the route? Fatalities. Injuries. The spectacle of a rescue helicopter head over teakettle down the slope. The first time I approached this crevasse from below, scampering up with my then-teenage brother, a large party descended out of the swirling fog, led by an ancient member of the Mazama Climbing Club. He took one look at us and howled, "Rope up, you damned tourists!" Which we did, unlike a friend of ours a few years later who, while descending the summit, was hit in the head with a rock the size of a basketball and knocked into the same crevasse. Not that a rope would have helped her much. Laurel survived, but only as a college-educated woman with the permanent mental capacity of a girl in the second grade.

So I know these things. But in my heart I do not believe them. In my heart I am still drawn to the mountains. "In the mountains," says T. S. Eliot, "there you feel free"—the only line of *The Waste Land* I have ever claimed to understand. And the mountains, the mountains that I have known. From the Alaska Range to the Juneau Icefield to the North Cascades to the Sierra Nevada to the lowly transverse ranges of the central coast of California, where I now live, I have loved them all. I live by glorious affirmation and denial.

It may be that this denial sometimes takes the form of my objecting to the more obvious risks that other climbers choose to take. In my mind I am the mountaineer who ropes up, who wears a helmet, who proceeds with caution, who turns back when necessary. I am not the one who brags about near-death experiences in *Outside* magazine. When my children were small, a climber friend and his climber wife, eight months pregnant, visited us in Santa Barbara. We went for a stroll one morning up a sandstone canyon outside the city, and all of a sudden Frank was aloft on the steep face of the canyon wall, a hundred feet off the deck. He had no rope. At lunch I asked him, "What the hell are you trying to prove?" For me, this was strong language. And that was the effective end of our friendship. But I seldom turn this outraged question on myself. Perhaps I do not want to risk alienating my own psyche.

Last month, when school got out, I went on what has now become an annual climb with another professor from my college. We hiked cross-country to a small Sierra tarn beneath a serrated, sinuous spur of Mt. Humphreys. There was a shorter and a longer version of this spur that we could try, and, aging achievers that we are, we talked ourselves into the longer route, gaining the crest two thousand feet beneath the summit. By late afternoon, after much roped climbing, we still had half the spur to go. Nearly out of water, time, and energy, we prudently but reluctantly decided to add Mt. Humphreys to our list of incomplete ascents. So we abandoned the crest and began our retreat, plunge-stepping down steep snow in a gully that dropped a thousand feet. Before long, my partner, feeling addled by the altitude, tripped and sailed blissfully downward, headfirst on his back. I felt the rope bend and tighten around my waist, and dug in my boots and my ax with what I hoped was alacrity. He bounced cleanly at the end of his tether and dangled there upside down, then slowly pulled himself to his feet.

"Thanks," he called.

"Don't mention it," I said.

The Wardrobe Wars

IN MY FRESHMAN YEAR at Wheaton College, back in the early seventies, the Wade Collection in Blanchard Hall acquired some new closet space—a wardrobe, to be exact. This wasn't a wardrobe that anyone actually used. It was just to look at, or perhaps to admire, or maybe even to worship. One student editorial in the campus paper suggested we cut slivers from the back of it and sell them as relics.

For this, of course, was not just any wardrobe, but one that had once belonged to C. S. Lewis, the unofficial patron saint of Wheaton College. And a beautiful piece of dark oak furniture it was—painstakingly handmade and elaborately handcarved by Lewis's grandfather and brought by Lewis from his boyhood home in Belfast to the Kilns, the house he shared with his brother, Warren, outside of Oxford. The college bought it at auction just after Warren died.

Other items of Lewis furniture from the Kilns were purchased by the college as well, including the obvious choice of a desk. But the wardrobe was particularly important because of its role in the first of the Chronicles of Narnia, *The Lion, the Witch, and the Wardrobe.* The wardrobe in the story is the threshold to fantasy; in the Wade Collection it became a tangible symbol of Lewis's powers as a writer, a sacrament of the literary imagination. It was the closest *thing* we had to Narnia.

The problem with literary relics, however, is that some Chaucerian Pardoner will always claim to have better ones. When I began teaching in the late eighties at Westmont College in Santa Barbara, I was surprised to see a somewhat plain but rather old wardrobe in the English Department across from our secretary's desk and not far from an equally old fireplace. On top of it lay a huge stuffed lion, which should have been my clue. This was the wardrobe, I was told. *The* wardrobe. (Surprising, isn't it, how definite that definite article sometimes becomes?) It had been obtained from the Kilns in 1975.

"But I thought the wardrobe was at Wheaton," I told my new colleagues.

"No way," they told me. "Wheaton's wardrobe is not even close to the one described in the story."

Then I was duly chaptered and versed by references to the sacred text. What the Pevensie children find in the empty room of the old Professor's country house is "one big wardrobe, the sort that has a looking glass in the door." I had to admit that the wardrobe before me was larger than the one I remembered from my undergraduate days, and that its door—its one door—was indeed covered with a looking glass. The Wheaton wardrobe, I was reminded, sadly lacked a looking glass on either of its two doors.

Once Lucy is left behind in the room, "she thought it would be worth while trying the door of the wardrobe, even though she felt almost sure that it would be locked." And sure enough, the Westmont wardrobe had a keyhole—as did the Wheaton wardrobe, if memory served me correctly. Inside the unlocked wardrobe, Lucy finds "a second row of coats hanging up behind the first one." This second row of coats is hanging on "hooks" or "pegs," and my colleagues opened the looking-glass door to point these out to me, hidden behind a first row of fur coats on hangers. The Wheaton wardrobe, I was told, might have hooks in the back as well (or were they pegs?), but did not have room for a row of hangers in front of them.

With the door thrown open, I was shown how easily Lucy could have "stepped into the wardrobe"—the threshold was just a foot off the floor. The Wheaton wardrobe, I was reminded, was more like a high-waisted cabinet. Lucy could only have *climbed* into it at best. Finally, my colleagues reminded me that the wardrobe in question had to be "a perfectly ordinary wardrobe," just like the one in the book. Did our wardrobe have any decorative carving? It did not. Wheaton had an ornate family heirloom, but it did not have the real thing.

Wardrobe closed. Case dismissed.

Has my alma mater been impressed by this impeccable brand of literary fundamentalism? Apparently not. According to one Wheaton brochure, theirs is the "wardrobe from which Lewis drew inspiration for *The Lion, the Witch and the Wardrobe*." And on the back of a postcard of the Wheaton wardrobe itself, we are likewise told that "according to Lewis's brother Warren, it was the inspiration for the wardrobe" in the celebrated novel. Old claims never die. They just grow more specific with time.

I was back at Wheaton for a conference just a couple of years ago. During a period of announcements, a curator from the Wade Collection invited the conference participants to visit the collection and see the many books and papers that had belonged to Lewis and his associates. At the end of her announcement, she told us, "We also have the wardrobe that served as the original for the one in the Narnia Chronicles."

There it was, that definite article again. In a remarkable display of maturity I put up my hand and said, "Excuse me, but *the* wardrobe is at Westmont College in Santa Barbara."

The woman gave me a long, hard look of the "we are not amused" variety. That was all. I wasn't able to find her after the session was over to clear things up.

Not that we could have, really. Of course, if pressed, I suspect we would both admit the wardrobe we are really concerned with exists only within the covers of a book, and that not even this wardrobe is so important as the story of which it is a part, and that the story is not so important as the sense of infinite longing that it stirs within our souls, and that this longing is not so important as the One—more real than Aslan himself—to whom it directs us. But that would be asking too much of either the curator or myself. To worship at our respective wardrobes, whether they be in Jerusalem or Samaria, is indeed to live in the shadowlands. And that is where we like it.

Lewis himself would doubtless say that the physical wardrobes in our possession are but copies of a faint copy. He might even claim, to our horror, that no single wardrobe inspired the one found in his book. Then he might add under his breath, like the

Professor in *The Last Battle* who has passed on to the next life, "It's all in Plato, all in Plato: bless me, what *do* they teach them at these schools!"

The reason that the Westmont wardrobe remained at the Kilns after the auction of other furniture was that it could not fit out the doorway of Joy Davidman's bedroom. The hall or door had been made smaller in the forties—and remember, it is a *large* wardrobe. The new owner of the house apparently cared little for Lewis and was prepared to destroy the wardrobe to make room for an American-style built-in closet. Walter Hooper, who has long served as Lewis's literary executor, reportedly thought it a great pity that the last remaining piece of furniture from Lewis's house should in all likelihood end up as firewood. That is when a group of Westmont students and faculty bought the wardrobe for next to nothing, had it dismantled, shipped it in pieces to Santa Barbara, and reassembled it carefully near the fireplace in Reynolds Hall.

But I have a little fantasy, thanks perhaps to Walter Hooper, about our wardrobe's proper end. Late some rainy California winter evening, long after my colleagues have returned to their homes and the students have slogged back up the hill to the residence halls, I will let myself back into the building, lock the doors, raise an ax high over my head, and with dolorous strokes split the wardrobe into kindling. Then I will stack the broken wood high in the old fireplace and start myself a cheerful blaze. By the light of this fire I will settle into a wingback chair, open a tattered book that was the first book to open me, and read far into the night.

About the Author

PAUL J. WILLIS is a professor of English at Westmont College in Santa Barbara, California. His poems, stories, essays and reviews have appeared in *The Best American Spiritual Writing 2004* (Houghton Mifflin), *The Best Spiritual Writing 1999* (HarperSanFrancisco), and in publications such as *Ascent, Books & Culture, The Christian Century, Image, Poetry, Redwood Coast Review, River Teeth* and *Wilderness.*

His most recent chapbooks of poetry are *Poison Oak* (Mille Grazie Press, 1999), *The Deep and Secret Color of Ice* (Small Poetry Press, 2003) and *How To Get There* (Finishing Line Press, 2004). He is also the author of two eco-fantasy novels, *No Clock in the Forest* and *The Stolen River* (both Avon, 1993). With David Starkey, he is co-editor of the anthology *In a Fine Frenzy: Poets Respond to Shakespeare* (University of Iowa Press, 2005). *Visiting Home,* his first full-length collection of poems, will be published by Pecan Grove Press in 2006.

Willis gives readings and workshops around the country. A former mountain guide in the Cascades and Sierra Nevada, he now spends his spare time rambling in the San Rafael Mountains behind his home.